the

ABCs

of
SAFE and HEALTHY
CHILD CARE

A Handbook for Child Care Providers

Department of Health and Human Services
U.S. Public Health Service
Centers for Disease Control and Prevention

ACKNOWLEDGMENTS

The authors wish to thank the following reviewers for their insightful suggestions and comments, which have greatly enhanced this handbook for child care providers.

Susan S. Aronson, M.D., F.A.A.P.
American Academy of Pediatrics, Pennsylvania Chapter

Janice Boase, R.N., M.S.
Seattle-King County Department of Public Health

Jo Cato, B.A.
State of Georgia

Peter Drabkin, M.P.H.
New York State Department of Health

Kathleen Gardner, B.S.N., M.A.T.
Chilton Memorial Hospital, New Jersey

Jan Gross, R.N., B.S.N.
Seattle-King County Department of Public Health

Pauline Koch, M.A.
National Association for Regulatory Administration

Carole Logan Kuhns, R.N., Ph.D.
Virginia Polytechnic Institute

Kristine L. MacDonald, M.D., M.P.H.
Council of State and Territorial Epidemiologists

Patricia M. Spahr, B.S., M.A.
National Association for the Education of Young Children

Yasmina Vinci, M.A., A.B.D.
National Association of Child Care Resource and Referral Agencies

Centers for Disease Control and Prevention
National Center for Infectious Diseases
Hospital Infections Program
Epidemiology Program Office

David Satcher, M.D., Ph.D., Director
James M. Hughes, M.D., Director
Martin S. Favero, Ph.D., Acting Director
Barbara R. Holloway, Deputy Director
and CDC Child Care Liaison

This handbook was prepared and produced by the **Hospital Infections Program**.

Authors:
Author/editor
Coauthor/editor

Cynthia M. Hale, B.A.
Jacquelyn A. Polder, B.S.N., M.P.H.

Editors:
Consulting editor
Consulting editor
Editor

Ralph L. Cordell, Ph.D.
Steven L. Solomon, M.D.
J Shaw

Graphics:
Public Health Practice Program Office
Cover Design and Illustrations artist
Orkand Corporation
Computer layout designer
Don Connelly and Associates
ABCs logo artist

Willie Richardson

Sheila R. Harding

Don Connelly

Major contributors:
Centers for Disease Control and Prevention
Epidemiology Program Office
National Center for Chronic Disease Prevention
and Health Promotion

National Center for Environmental Health

National Center for HIV, STD, and TB Prevention

National Center for Injury Prevention and Control
National Immunization Program
National Institute for Occupational Health and Safety

R. Elliott Churchill, M.A.

Bettylou Sherry, Ph.D., R.D.
Barbara Z. Park, R.D.H., M.P.H.
Elizabeth H. Donnelly, C.H.P.
Carol A. Pertowski, M.D.
Camille Smith, M.S., Ed.S.
John A. Jereb, M.D.
Robert J. Simonds, M.D.
Jeffrey J. Sacks, M.D.
Mark Papania, M.D.
Naomi G. Swanson, Ph.D.

Environmental Protection Agency
Office of Radiation and Indoor Air

Laura Kolb, B.A., M.P.H.

Table of Contents

INTRODUCTION

The Centers for Disease Control and Prevention (CDC) has written this handbook to help you, the child care provider, reduce sickness, injury, and other health problems in your child care facility. The information in this handbook applies to any child care provider in any setting, whether you take care of children in a center or in your own home.

This handbook revises and updates the previous CDC handbook, *What to Do to Stop Disease in Child Day Care Centers*, which is now out of print.

WHAT YOUR HANDBOOK INCLUDES

This handbook will help you maintain a safe and healthy child care setting, with up-to-date information, including:

- How infectious diseases are spread.
- What you can do to keep yourself and the children in your care healthy.
- What disease and injury prevention practices you should follow.
- What disease and injury prevention practices you should require parents to follow.
- What the most common childhood diseases and health conditions are, how to recognize them, and what you can do when they occur.

HOW DISEASES SPREAD

Infectious diseases are caused by germs, such as viruses, bacteria, and parasites. Contagious or communicable diseases are those that can be spread from one person to another. Infectious diseases that commonly occur among children are often communicable or contagious and may spread very easily from person to person.

Infants and toddlers are highly susceptible to contagious diseases. They have not yet been exposed to many of the most common germs. Therefore, they have not yet built up resistance or immunity to them. Also, young children have many habits that promote the spread of germs. For example, they often put their fingers and other objects in their mouths. In this way, germs enter and leave the body and can then infect the child or be passed on to others.

In order for germs to be spread from one person to another, three things must happen.

(1) Germs must be present in the environment, either through a person carrying the germ or through infectious body fluids, such as discharge from the eye, nose, mouth, or digestive (gastrointestinal) tract; in the air; or on a surface.

(2) A person who is not immune to the germ must come in contact with or be exposed to the germs.

(3) The contact or exposure must be in a way that leads to infection.

2

How Some Childhood Infectious Diseases Are Spread

Method of Transmission			
Direct Contact with infected person's skin or body fluid	Respiratory Transmission (passing from the lungs, throat, or nose of one person to another person through the air)	Fecal-Oral Transmission (touching feces or objects contaminated with feces then touching your mouth)	Blood Transmission
Chickenpox* Cold Sores Conjunctivitis Head Lice Impetigo Ringworm Scabies	Chickenpox* Common Cold Diphtheria Fifth Disease Bacterial meningitis* Hand-Foot-Mouth Disease Impetigo Influenza* Measles* Mumps* Pertussis* Pneumonia Rubella*	Campylobacter** E. Coli O157** Enterovirus Giardia Hand-Foot-Mouth Disease Hepatitis A* Infectious Diarrhea Pinworms Polio* Salmonella** Shigella	Cytomegalovirus Hepatitis B* Hepatitis C HIV Infection

*Vaccines are available for preventing these diseases.
**Often transmitted from infected animals through foods or direct contact.

As the table shows.

- Skin infections may be spread by touching fluid from another person's infected sores.
- Respiratory-tract infections with symptoms such as coughs, sneezes, and runny noses are spread mainly through exposure to fluids present in or expelled from another person's mouth and throat (saliva or mucus), often when an uninfected person touches these discharges with their hands and then touches their mouth, eyes, or nose.
- Intestinal tract infections, including some types of diarrhea, usually are spread through exposure to germs in the feces. Many of the germs discussed in this manual are spread through what is known as "fecal-oral" transmission. This means that germs leave the body of the infected person in the feces (poop) and enter the body of another person through the mouth. In most situations, this happens when objects (including toys, fingers, or hands) which have become contaminated with undetectable amounts of feces are placed in the mouth. Fecal-oral transmission can also occur if food or water is contaminated with undetectable amounts of human or animal feces, and then is eaten or drunk. Improperly prepared foods made from animals (for example, meat, milk, and eggs) are often the source of infection with *Campylobacter*, *E.coli O157*, and *Salmonella*.
- Some infections, like infection with *Salmonella* and *Campylobacter*, may be spread through direct exposure to infected animals.
- Blood infections are spread when blood (and sometimes other body fluids) from a person with an infection gets into the bloodstream of an uninfected person. This can happen when infected blood or body fluid enters the body of an uninfected person through cuts or openings in the skin; the mucous membrane that lines body cavities, such as the nose and eye; or directly into the bloodstream, as with a needle.
- Some diseases, such as chickenpox, impetigo, and hand-foot-and mouth disease, can have more than one transmission route. For example, they may be spread through air or by direct contact with the infectious germ.

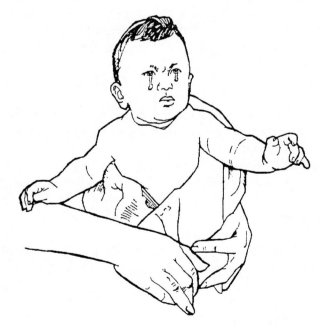

INJURIES IN THE CHILD CARE SETTING

The risk of an injury happening is directly related to the physical environment and children's behaviors, and how these are managed. Injuries can be divided into two categories--unintentional and intentional. Unintentional injuries may result from choking, falls, burns, drowning, swallowing toxic or other materials (poisoning), cuts from sharp objects. exposure to environmental hazards such as chemicals, radon, or lead, or animal bites, or other "accidents." (Some of the common environmental hazards are addressed in the "Maintaining a Safe and Healthy Child Care Facility" section of this booklet.) Intentional injuries are usually due to bites, fights, or abuse.

Preventing Injuries

You can prevent most injuries that occur in the child care setting by:

- Supervising children carefully.
- Checking the child care and play areas for, and getting rid of, hazards.
- Using safety equipment for children. such as car seats and seat belts, bicycle helmets, and padding, such as for the knees and elbows.
- Understanding what children can do at different stages of development. Children learn by testing their abilities. They should be allowed to participate in activities appropriate for their development even though these activities may result in some minor injuries, such as scrapes and bruises. However, children should be prevented from taking part in activities or using equipment that is beyond their abilities and that may result in major injuries such as broken bones.
- Teaching children how to use playground equipment safely (e.g., going down the slide feet first).

Preparing for Injuries

Injuries require immediate action. You will need to assess the injury to determine what type of medical attention, if any, is required. Everyone working with children should have up-to-date training in first aid and cardiopulmonary resuscitation (CPR). At a minimum, one person with this training must be present at the child care site at all times. The next chapter on "Establishing Policies to Promote Health and Safety" includes a section on policies you should use to handle injuries and other emergencies.

Unintentional Injuries

Children are often injured unintentionally during the normal course of a day. Many of these injuries, such as scrapes and bruises, are minor and only need simple first aid. Other injuries can be serious and require medical attention beyond first aid. Call 911 or your local emergency number if an injured child has any of the following conditions:
- severe neck or head injury,
- choking,
- severe bleeding,
- shock,
- chemicals in eyes, on skin, or ingested in the mouth. or
- near-drowning.

See the first aid chart in the next chapter for what actions to take for some common injuries.

Hazards in the Facility

Children in child care have many opportunities for coming in contact with substances that can hurt them. Child care providers can help reduce children's exposure to these hazards by taking preventive measures. Chapter III, on "Maintaining a Safe and Healthy Facility," gives information on preventing children's exposure to such harmful substances as chemicals, lead, air pollution, and radon in the child care setting.

Intentional Injuries
Aggressive Behavior and Bites

Children show aggression (hostile, injurious, or destructive behavior) either verbally (what they say) or physically (how they act). Verbal aggression by other children or adults, such as belittling, ridiculing, or taunting a child, can injure a child's self-esteem. Physical aggression, such as biting, hitting, scratching, and kicking, may result in physical injuries. Parents have become greatly concerned about physical injuries that cause bleeding to their child, especially being bitten by another child, because they fear this may expose their child to a risk of infection from HIV, which causes AIDS, or hepatitis B virus, which can cause liver damage.

To deter aggressive behavior you should:

- Set clear limits for children's behavior. Explain those limits to both children and their parents.
- Explain to a child who is showing aggressive behavior how the aggressive actions affect the victim.
- Redirect a child's aggressive behavior by, for example, engaging the child in a sport or activity that interests the child.
- Teach and reinforce coping skills.
- Encourage children to express feelings verbally, in a healthy way.
- Provide acceptable opportunities for children to release anger. Running outside, kicking balls, punching bags, and other physical play allows children to let off steam.

If a child is bitten by another child:

- Administer first aid.
- Ask the parents of the injured child to seek medical care if the bite causes bleeding.
- Notify the parents of both children if the bite causes bleeding. Testing the children for HIV or hepatitis B may be considered and should be discussed with the health care providers of both children involved.

A child who is known to be positive for HIV or hepatitis B AND who bites, even after efforts to change the behavior, should be taken out of the child care setting until the biting ceases.

Child Abuse

Child abuse is harm to, or neglect of, a child by another person, whether adult or child. Child abuse happens in all cultural, ethnic, and income groups. Child abuse can be physical, emotional/verbal, sexual or through neglect. Abuse may cause serious injury to the child and may even result in death. Signs of possible abuse include:

Physical Abuse

Unexplained or repeated injuries such as welts, bruises, or burns.
Injuries that are in the shape of an object (belt buckle, electric cord, etc.)
Injuries not likely to happen given the age or ability of the child. For example, broken bones in a child   too young to walk or climb.
Disagreement between the child's and the parent's explanation of the injury.
Unreasonable explanation of the injury.
Obvious neglect of the child (dirty, undernourished, inappropriate clothes for the weather, lack of medical   or dental care).
Fearful behavior.

Emotional/Verbal Abuse

Aggressive or withdrawn behavior.
Shying away from physical contact with parents or adults.
Afraid to go home.

Sexual Abuse

Child tells you he/she was sexually mistreated.
Child has physical signs such as:
  difficulty in walking or sitting.
  stained or bloody underwear.
  genital or rectal pain, itching, swelling, redness, or discharge
  bruises or other injuries in the genital or rectal area.
Child has behavioral and emotional signs such as:
  difficulty eating or sleeping.
  soiling or wetting pants or bed after being potty trained.
  acting like a much younger child.
  excessive crying or sadness.
  withdrawing from activities and others.
  talking about or acting out sexual acts beyond normal sex play for age.

Abuse can happen in any family, regardless of any special characteristics. However, in dealing with parents, be aware of characteristics of families in which abuse may be more likely:
- Families who are isolated and have no friends, relatives, church or other support systems.
- Parents who tell you they were abused as children.
- Families who are often in crisis (have money problems, move often).
- Parents who abuse drugs or alcohol.
- Parents who are very critical of their child.

- Parents who are very rigid in disciplining their child.
- Parents who show too much or too little concern for their child.
- Parents who feel they have a difficult child.
- Parents who are under a lot of stress.

If you suspect child abuse of any kind, you should:
- Take the child to a quiet, private area.
- Gently encourage the child to give you enough information to evaluate whether abuse may have occurred.
- Remain calm so as not to upset the child.
- If the child reveals the abuse, reassure him/her that you believe him/her, that he/she is right to tell you, and that he/she is not bad.
- Tell the child you are going to talk to persons who can help him/her.
- Return the child to the group (if appropriate).
- Record all information.
- Immediately report the suspected abuse to the proper local authorities. In most states, reporting suspected abuse is required by law.

If you employ other providers or accept volunteers to help you care for the children in your facility, you should check their background for a past history of child abuse or other criminal activity. Contact your local police department. Many states require that child care providers have background and criminal history checks.

Dealing with child abuse is emotionally difficult for a provider. As a child care provider, you should get training in recognizing and reporting child abuse before you are confronted with a suspected case. If you suspect a case of child abuse, you may need to seek support from your local health department, child support services department, or other sources within your area.

8

ESTABLISHING POLICIES TO PROMOTE HEALTH AND SAFETY

CDC recommends that you establish and follow certain policies in order to set up and keep a safe and healthy child care setting. You need to be able to explain to parents why the policies are important. You need to remind yourself and parents of these policies on a regular basis. Your state, county, or city may have regulations and laws that you must follow. This handbook does not take the place of your state's or locality's child care regulations and laws. **In every case, the laws and regulations of the city, county, and state in which the child care facility is located must be carefully followed even if they differ from recommendations in this manual.**

CDC recommends that you establish written policies about the following topics. Each of these policies will be described later in this section.

Health History and Immunizations for Children in Child Care
Health History and Immunizations for Providers of Child Care
Exclusion for Illness
Reporting Requirements
Emergency Illness or Injury Procedures
Children with Special Needs
Medication Administration
Nutrition/Foods Brought From Home
No Smoking or Use of Alcohol or Illegal Drugs

In developing policies, you should make sure that you:

- Have the equipment and supplies necessary to make the policies work.
- Organize the facility to support the policies.
- Use proper procedures to support the policies.
- Keep lines of communication open with everyone involved-- staff members, parents, and children.
- Assure that all staff, parents, and others are educated regarding the policies, as appropriate.

To prevent the spread of contagious diseases, recommended policies and procedures must be followed AT ALL TIMES because:
- People can spread an infection to other people before showing any symptoms of illness.
- People can carry and spread germs without ever getting sick themselves.
- In a child care setting, where people from different families spend many hours together in close physical contact, germs are spread more easily.

HEALTH HISTORY AND IMMUNIZATION POLICY
FOR CHILDREN IN CHILD CARE

You need to know the health history of, and medical emergency information for, every child in your care. When a child enrolls in your child care facility, you should find out:

- Where parents can be reached--full names and work and home phone numbers and addresses.
- At least 2 people to contact if parents can't be reached--phone numbers and addresses.
- The child's regular health care providers--names, addresses, and phone numbers.
- The hospital that the child's family uses--name, address, and phone number.
- The date of the child's last physical examination. Any child who has not had a well baby or well child examination recently (within the past 6 months for children under 2 years old and within 1 year for those 2 to 6 years old) should be examined within 30 days of entering your child care facility.

- Any special health problems or medical conditions that a child may have and procedures to follow to deal with these conditions. Examples of conditions needing procedures are allergies, asthma, diabetes, epilepsy, and sickle cell anemia. These conditions can cause sudden attacks that may require immediate action. You should know 1) what happens to the child during a crisis related to the condition, 2) how to prevent a crisis, 3) how to deal with a crisis, and 4) whether you need training in a particular emergency procedure.
- The child's vaccination status.
- Whether the child has been evaluated with a TB skin test (using the Mantoux method with tuberculin purified protein derivative (PPD)).

You should require that all children admitted to your care be up to date on their vaccinations. Laws in many states require you to have written proof of each child's up-to-date vaccinations. Children attending child care especially need all of the recommended vaccinations to protect themselves, the other children, the child care provider, and their families. Several diseases that can cause serious problems for children and adults can be prevented by vaccination. These diseases are chicken pox, diphtheria, *Haemophilus influenzae* meningitis, hepatitis A, hepatitis B, influenza, measles, mumps, polio, rubella (German measles or 3-day measles), tetanus, and whooping cough (pertussis). Many of these diseases are becoming less common because most people have been vaccinated against them. But cases still occur and children in child care are at increased risk for many of these diseases because of the many hours they spend in close contact with other children.

Children who are not up to date on their vaccinations should be taken out of child care (excluded) until they have begun the series of shots needed. In the absence of an outbreak, they may usually continue to attend child care as long as they continue to receive the shots as recommended. Many states require that children whose vaccinations are not up to date be excluded from group care. Each child in your care should have a certificate of up-to-date immunization in your files. In many states this is a legal requirement and blank certificates are supplied by the state. Georgia's certificate is shown on the next page.

Front of form:

Georgia Department of Human Resources
PRE-SCHOOL/CHILD CARE IMMUNIZATION CERTIFICATE

Name of Child (Last, First, Middle)　　　　Parent or Guardian

Date of Birth　　　　Date of *MMR*　　　　*Month and Year Next Immunization Due*
(This certificate expires at the end of the month shown)

___ *Medical Exemption (Long Term Condition)*

Name of Licensed Physician or　　　___ *Religious*　　　___ *School*
Health Department　　　　　　　　　　　*Exemption*　　　　*Exemption*

School Attending

Signature　　　　　　　　　　Signature of Facility Director

Date of Certification　　　　　　Date of Certification

Form 3227 (Rev. 8-94)　　　*SEE THE OTHER SIDE OF THIS FORM FOR EXPLANATION OF ITS USES.*

Back of form:

Operators of all public and private facilities intended for the care, supervision or instruction of children are required by law to keep on file a certificate of immunization for each child who attends. (Section 20-2-771, Official Code of Georgia, Annotated) Schools (Kindergarten through twelfth grade; ages 5-19) use DHR Form 3032. All other facilities use this form.

A doctor of medicine or osteopathy or a health department official may certify immunizations by entering a date for ***MONTH AND YEAR NEXT IMMUNIZATION DUE*** if a child is being immunized against diphtheria, tetanus, pertussis, haemophilus influenza type B disease, and polio in accord with standard immunization practices; and if the child is older than 15 months and has been immunized against measles, mumps, and rubella.

A doctor of medicine or osteopathy or a health department official may check the box for ***Medical Exemption*** if there are long term medical reasons that immunizations might be harmful to the child. A medical exemption does not expire until a doctor decides it is safe to immunize.

The director of a pre-school/child-care facility may check the box for ***School Exemption*** and complete the certification if a child is at least 5 years old and is known to be attending a school. The director may check the box for ***Religious Exemption*** only if a valid affidavit of religious conflict has been received from a parent.

To Reorder: Georgia Department of Human Resources
Immunization Program, Room 10-220
Two Peachtree Street, N.W.
Atlanta, Georgia 30303-3186

Form 3227 (Rev. 8-94)　　　(Reverse Side)

12

The certificate should state that the child is up to date for immunizations. list the date when the next immunization is due (the date the certificate expires), and be signed by the child's health care provider. As the date when the next immunization is due approaches, you should remind the child's parents of the pending immunization and request a new immunization certificate. If the child is exempt from vaccination because of a medical condition or religious objection, this should be noted on the immunization certificate and supported in the child's file with documentation from the physician or religious authority. Many states include the date of each immunization on the immunization certificate. Rapid access to this information can be very useful during an outbreak.

The following table lists the current recommended schedule for routine immunization of infants and children. Because this schedule changes frequently, you should contact your local health department for annual updates.

Recommended Childhood Immunization Schedule United States, July - December 1996

Vaccines are listed under the routinely recommended ages. Bars indicate range of acceptable ages for vaccination. Shaded bars indicate catch-up vaccination: at 11-12 years of age, hepatitis B vaccine should be administered to children not previously vaccinated, and Varicella Zoster Virus vaccine should be administered to children not previously vaccinated who lack a reliable history of chickenpox.

Age ▶ Vaccine ▼	Birth	1 mo	2 mos	4 mos	6 mos	12 mos	15 mos	18 mos	4-6 yrs	11-12 yrs	14-16 yrs
Hepatitis B[1,2]	Hep B-1		Hep B-2		Hep B-3					Hep B[2]	
Diphtheria, Tetanus, Pertussis[3]			DTP	DTP	DTP	DTP[3] (DTaP at 15+ m)			DTP or DTaP	Td	
H. influenzae type b[4]			Hib	Hib	Hib[4]	Hib[4]					
Polio[5]			OPV[5]	OPV	OPV				OPV		
Measles, Mumps, Rubella[6]						MMR			MMR[6] or MMR[6]		
Varicella Zoster Virus Vaccine[7]						Var				Var[7]	

Approved by the Advisory Committee on Immunization Practices (ACIP), the American Academy of Pediatrics (AAP), and the American Academy of Family Physicians (AAFP).

HEALTH HISTORY AND IMMUNIZATION POLICY
FOR CHILD CARE PROVIDERS

Children, especially those in groups, are more likely to get infectious diseases than are adults. As a child care provider, you will be exposed to infectious diseases more frequently than will someone who has less contact with children. To protect yourself and children in your care, you need to know what immunizations you received as a child and whether you had certain childhood diseases. If you are not sure, your health care provider can test your blood to determine if you are immune to some of these diseases and can vaccinate you against those to which you are not immune. The Advisory Committee on Immunization Practices has not developed official recommendations for vaccination of child care providers. The table on the next page lists the immunizations that CDC believes are appropriate for child care providers, based on the official recommendations for vaccination of adults in other occupations and settings.

Tuberculosis Screening

Persons who are beginning work as child care providers should have a TB skin test (Mantoux method using tuberculin purified protein derivative (PPD)) to check for infection with the TB germ, unless there is documentation of a positive test result in the past or of active TB that has been treated already. The first time that they are tested, persons who cannot document any previous TB skin test results should have a two-step test. (That is, if the first test result is negative, the skin test is repeated within one month.) Persons who have negative results from their skin tests when they start child care work should have their skin tests repeated every 2 years while the results are still negative. Also, in family home child care settings, all persons aged 12 years and older who are present while the children are there should receive TB skin tests under this same schedule, even if they are not providing child care.

Anyone who has a positive result from the skin test may be infected with the TB germ and should be evaluated promptly by a physician, who will check for active TB. Regardless of TB skin test results, persons who have symptoms of active TB, such as a cough that "won't go away," coughing up blood, weight loss, night sweats, or tiredness should not attend, work, or volunteer at a child care facility until they have been evaluated by a physician. Persons who have active TB should not return to a child care setting until the local health department has determined that they are no longer contagious.

Recommended Immunization Schedule for Child Care Providers

Immunization	How Often	Why
Influenza	All child care providers, especially those who have chronic health conditions or are over 65 years of age should be vaccinated against influenza. Vaccination is given yearly, in October or November (before the flu season), because a new influenza vaccine is developed each year to protect against the viruses expected that year.	Influenza causes fever, chills, headache, muscle ache, sore throat, cough, and cold symptoms. Influenza may lead to pneumonia and other severe illness among the elderly and those with chronic illnesses or weak immune systems.
Measles, Mumps, Rubella (MMR)	Child care providers should be immune to measles, mumps, and rubella. Providers born before 1957 can be considered immune to measles and mumps. Others can be considered immune if they have a history of measles or mumps disease or have received at least one dose of rubella vaccine on or after their first birthday. Because a history of rubella disease is often unreliable, only a blood test indicating Immunity to rubella or documented receipt of at least one dose of rubella vaccine is adequate proof of immunity. Measles, mumps, and rubella vaccines are usually given together as MMR. Many experts recommend two doses of MMR for persons without other evidence of immunity.	Measles: 2-3 people out of every 1,000 who contract measles die from complications such as pneumonia or encephalitis. Encephalitis is an inflammation of the brain, which can lead to convulsions, deafness, or mental retardation. Measles during pregnancy increases the risk of premature labor, spontaneous abortion, and low birth weight. Mumps: 15% of cases are in adolescents and adults. Mumps may cause inflammation of the pancreas or sexual organs and may cause permanent deafness or sterility. Rubella: 15% of young adults are susceptible. Rubella may cause miscarriage, stillbirth, and multiple birth defects (congenital disorders, mental retardation) if contracted in the first trimester of pregnancy.
Tetanus, Diphtheria (Td)	Child care providers should have a record of receiving a series of 3 doses (usually given in childhood) and a booster dose given within the past 10 years.	Tetanus (lockjaw) causes painful muscular contractions. 40%-50% of persons who contract tetanus die. Diphtheria affects throat and nasal passages, interferes with breathing, and produces a toxin that damages the heart, kidneys, and nerves. 10% of cases are fatal.

Immunization	How Often	Why
Polio	Child care providers, especially those working with children who are not toilet-trained, should have a record of a primary series of 3 doses (usually given in childhood) and a supplementary dose given at least 6 months after the third dose in the primary series.	Polio attacks the nervous system and can cause paralysis in legs or other areas. When children are vaccinated using live polio vaccine, they may shed live polio vaccine virus in their feces or urine for several weeks after receiving the vaccine. Very rarely, the vaccine virus can change into a more dangerous form and cause paralytic polio. Anyone who is in frequent contact with recently vaccinated children, especially changing diapers, should be certain she or he has been vaccinated against polio.
Hepatitis A	Hepatitis A vaccine is not routinely recommended for child care providers but may be indicated if the local health department determines that the risk of hepatitis A in the community is high. Any person who travels frequently should consider getting hepatitis A vaccine.	Hepatitis A is a liver infection that causes fever, a loss of appetite, nausea, diarrhea, and generally ill feeling that may persist for weeks. During an outbreak in a child care setting, hepatitis A spreads easily and quickly. However, in the absence of an outbreak, the risk to child care providers in general does not seem to be increased.
Chickenpox	Child care providers who know they have had chicken pox can assume they are immune. All other providers should consider getting vaccinated against chicken-pox because of the high risk of exposure to chickenpox. Persons who believe they have never had chickenpox or are unsure can be vaccinated. In some areas, blood tests may be available to determine if a person is susceptible and in need of vaccination.	Chickenpox can be a severe disease in adults. Child care providers are at high risk of being exposed to chickenpox in the child care setting.
Hepatitis B	Child care providers who may have contact with blood or blood-contaminated body fluids or who work with developmentally disabled or aggressive children should be vaccinated against hepatitis B with one series of 3 doses of vaccine.	Hepatitis B causes serious illness and 1 in 20 persons will develop chronic hepatitis, which can destroy the liver and raise the risk of getting liver cancer. Persons who develop chronic hepatitis B are infectious to others for the rest of their life.

Provider Exclusion/Readmittance Criteria

A child care provider should be temporarily excluded from providing care to children if she or he has one or more of the following conditions.

Condition	Exclude from Child Care Facility
Chickenpox	Until 6 days after the start of rash or when sores have dried/crusted.
Shingles	Only if sores cannot be covered by clothing or a dressing; if not, exclude until sores have crusted and are dry. A person with active shingles should not care for immune suppressed children.
Rash with fever or joint pain	Until diagnosed not to be measles or rubella.
Measles	Until 5 days after rash starts.
Rubella	Until 6 days after rash starts.
Mumps	Until 9 days after glands begin to swell.
Diarrheal illness	If 3 or more episodes of loose stools during previous 24 hours, or if diarrhea is accompanied by fever, until diarrhea resolves.
Vomiting	If 2 or more episodes of vomiting during the previous 24 hours, or if accompanied by a fever, until vomiting resolves or is determined to be due to such noninfectious conditions as pregnancy or digestive disorder.
Hepatitis A	For 1 week after jaundice appears or as directed by health department, especially when no symptoms are present.
Pertussis	Until after 5 days of antibiotic therapy.
Impetigo (a skin infection)	Until 24 hours after antibiotic treatment begins and lesions are not draining.
Active Tuberculosis (TB)	Until the local health department approves return to the facility.
Strep throat (or other Streptococcal infection)	Until 24 hours after initial antibiotic treatment and fever has ended.
Scabies/head lice/etc.	Until 24 hours after treatment has begun.
Purulent conjunctivitis	Until 24 hours after treatment has begun.
Other conditions mandated by state public health law.	As required by law (consult your local health department).

Health Risks for Pregnant Child Care Providers

Knowing your health history is especially important if you are pregnant or could become pregnant and are providing child care. Several childhood diseases can harm the unborn child, or fetus, of a pregnant woman exposed to these diseases for the first time. These diseases are:

- Chickenpox or Shingles (Varicella Virus)--First-time exposure to this virus during pregnancy may cause miscarriage, multiple birth defects, severe disease in newborns. Chickenpox can be a serious illness in adults. Most people (90% to 95% of adults) were exposed to chickenpox as children and are immune. For women who do not know if they had chickenpox as a child, a blood test can verify if they are immune. If they are not immune, a chickenpox vaccine is now available. Vaccination against chickenpox before you get pregnant may reduce the risk of passing the virus to your fetus should you become pregnant in the future and then are exposed to chickenpox. Because the vaccine may harm a fetus, the vaccine is not given to pregnant women. Your physician will ask you if you are pregnant before giving you the vaccination and will advise you to avoid pregnancy for 1 month following each dose of vaccine.

- Cytomegalovirus (CMV)--First-time exposure to CMV during pregnancy may cause hearing loss, seizures, mental retardation, deafness, and/or blindness in the newborn. In the United States, cytomegalovirus is a common infection passed from mother to child at birth. Providers who care for children under 2 years of age are at increased risk of exposure to CMV. Most people (and 40% to 70% of women of childbearing age) have been exposed to CMV and are immune. There is no licensed vaccine against CMV.

- Fifth Disease (erythema infectiosum)--First-time exposure to fifth disease during pregnancy may increase the risk of fetal damage or death. Most people (and 30% to 60% of women of childbearing age) have been exposed to the virus and are immune. There is no vaccine licensed for fifth disease.

- Rubella (German or 3-day measles)--First-time exposure to rubella during the first 3 months of pregnancy may cause fetal deafness, cataracts, heart damage, mental retardation, miscarriage, or stillbirth. Rubella can also be a severe illness in adults. Everyone who works in a child care facility should have proof of immunity to rubella on file at the facility. Child care providers can be considered immune only if (a) they have had a blood test for rubella antibodies and the laboratory report shows antibodies or (b) they have been vaccinated against rubella on or after their first birthday. Providers who are not immune should be vaccinated. Because it is not known whether the vaccine may harm a fetus, a woman should not be vaccinated if she is pregnant. After vaccination, a woman should avoid getting pregnant for 3 months.

EXCLUSION FOR ILLNESS

As a child care provider, you will need a clearly written policy for excluding sick children from your child care facility. Give each parent and guardian a copy of your Exclusion for Illness Policy when each child is enrolled. Explain the policy and answer any questions that the parents or guardians have at that time. This will prevent problems later when a child is sick.

Children can become sick quickly. You should be aware of signs and symptoms of illness and know what to do if a child becomes ill. You should have a procedure for recording in writing and reporting any unusual illness or injury.

Each day when the children arrive at your facility you should:

- Check the overall health of each child. Note any unusual symptoms and ask parents or guardians about any unusual health or behavior while the child was not in your care.
- If a child does not appear well enough to participate in activities as usual and/or has any symptoms requiring removal from the child care setting (see below), the child should not be allowed to attend the child care facility at that time.

18

You should continue to watch each child's health throughout the day while in your care. Because infections spread easily among children, you should look for the symptoms requiring removal of a child from a child care setting (see below). If you see these symptoms in a child, you should:

- Immediately separate the child from the other children.
- Contact the parents to have the child picked up.
- Continue to observe the child for other symptoms.
- If the child does not respond to you, is having trouble breathing, or is having a convulsion, call 911.

Symptoms Requiring Removal of a Child from the Child Care Setting

- **Fever**--AND sore throat, rash, vomiting, diarrhea, earache, irritability, or confusion. Fever is defined as having a temperature of 100°F or higher taken under the arm, 101°F taken orally, or 102°F taken rectally. For children 4 months or younger, the lower rectal temperature of 101° is considered a fever threshold.
- **Diarrhea**--runny, watery, or bloody stools
- **Vomiting**--2 or more times in a 24-hour period.
- **Body rash with fever.**
- **Sore throat with fever and swollen glands.**
- **Severe coughing**--child gets red or blue in the face or makes high-pitched whooping sound after coughing.
- **Eye discharge**--thick mucus or pus draining from the eye, or pink eye.
- **Yellowish skin or eyes.**
- **Child is irritable, continuously crying, or requires more attention that you can provide without hurting the health and safety of other children in your care.**

REPORTING REQUIREMENTS

When you know that a child has a specific disease, you may need to take control measures so that the disease does not spread to others. Some diseases or conditions must be reported to the local health department. Child care providers should contact their local health department to find out what diseases they need to report. You may want to inform parents of these requirements in "parent information" packages.

When you are required to report certain diseases to the health department, you should do so promptly, even if the sick child is under the care of his or her own physician. The physician, who is also required to report the occurrence of these diseases to local health authorities, may not do so, or the physician may not know that the child is attending child care. The health department needs to know a child is in child care in order to determine appropriate preventive measures. These might include watching the other children in the child care home or center for signs of illness and giving them preventive treatment, if necessary. Suspected child abuse or neglect must also be reported. The agency to which you report abuse and neglect varies by locality. The agency may be the police department, the department of family and child services, child protective services, or others. Check with the local authorities in your area to identify the appropriate reporting agency. You also should inform parents of this reporting requirement.

The table on the next few pages summarizes actions that CDC recommends that you take if you know a child in your care has been diagnosed with one of the diseases that commonly occur in a child care setting. The table also tells you when to allow the sick child to return to the child care setting after being excluded.

20

EXCLUSION/READMISSION DUE TO ILLNESS

Disease	If a Child in Your Care Has Been Diagnosed With This Disease You Should	When to Allow Child to Return
Bacterial Meningitis	•Exclude the child from child care. (In most cases, the child will be hospitalized.) •Immediately contact your Health Department to report the case of meningitis. They will contact the child's physician and make recommendations about what to do to prevent the spread of infection.. 　—Ask whether you need to contact the parents of the other children in your facility. The Health Department may recommend antibiotics for children and adults in the facility. •If so, in cooperation with the Health Department, contact the parents of the children in your facility and tell them: 　—that their child may have been exposed to meningitis. 　—that their child should see a physician IMMEDIATELY if fever, headache, rashes, spots, unusual behavior, or any other symptom that concerns them develops. 　—to follow any preventive measures the Health Department recommends. •Carefully follow group separation and good hygiene procedures. (See chapter on Protective Practices.)	When the Health Department tells you it is safe.
Chickenpox	•Temporarily exclude the sick child from the child care setting. •Notify parents, especially those whose child is 　—taking steroid medications. 　—being treated with cancer or leukemia drugs. 　—is immunosuppressed. (Chickenpox can be extremely dangerous to these children.) •You may contact your Health Department to find out what other preventive measures to take. •Carefully follow group separation, handwashing, and cleaning procedures. (See chapter on Protective Practices.)	6 days after the rash begins or when blisters have scabbed over.
Diarrheal Disease	•Temporarily exclude the sick child from the child care setting. •Carefully follow group separation, handwashing, and cleaning procedures. (See chapter on Protective Practices.) •If you know the diarrhea is caused by bacteria or a parasite such as shigella, campylobacter, *E. coli, Cryptosporidium,* salmonella, or giardia, ask the Health Department 　—whether other ill and well children and adults should be tested. 　—when to allow the sick child to return to child care.	When the child no longer has diarrhea. However, some of these diseases require negative stool cultures; allow the child to return when the Health Depart-ment tells you it is safe.
Diphtheria	•Temporarily exclude the sick child from the child care setting. •Immediately contact the Health Department to ask what additional preventive measures should be taken. •Observe all children and adults for sore throats for 7 days. •Anyone developing a sore throat should see a physician. •Advise parents that their child should see a physician if 　—the child develops a sore throat. 　—the child is incompletely immunized against diphtheria. •Carefully follow group separation and good hygiene procedures. (See chapter on "Protective Practices.")	When the Health Department tells you it is safe.

Disease	If a Child in Your Care Has Been Diagnosed With This Disease You Should	When to Allow Child to Return

Epiglottitis	•A child diagnosed with this disease will probably be hospitalized.
	Contact your Health Department and ask what preventive measures to take.
	—The Health Department may tell you to contact all parents and tell them
	    (1) that their children may have been exposed to a serious contagious disease,
	    (2) that their children should immediately see a physician if they develop *fever, headache, symptoms of infection, or behavior that seems unusual* and
	    (3) about any additional preventive measures the Health Department has recommended.
	•Carefully follow group separation and good hygiene procedures.
	IMPORTANT: *H-flu* is not the same germ as "flu" or influenza. *H-flu* can cause SERIOUS ILLNESS in young children. If a case of *H-flu* occurs in your facility, TAKE ALL ACTIONS ABOVE.
		Not due to *H-flu*: When treating physician tells you it is safe.
		
		Due to *H-flu*: When the Health Department tells you it is safe.

Hand- Foot- and- Mouth Disease	•Exclude if child has open, draining lesion on hand or has lesions in the mouth AND is drooling.	When lesions heal or drooling ceases.
Head Lice	•Temporarily exclude the infested child from the child care setting. •Contact your Health Department or health consultant for advice about examining, treating, and readmitting exposed children and adults. •Check the other children for lice or nits (eggs of lice).	24 hours after treatment.
Hepatitis A	•Temporarily exclude the sick child from the child care setting. •Immediately notify your Health Department. (They may recommend immune globulin shots and possibly vaccination for children and adults and additional preventive measures.) Ask for specific recommendations on notifying parents and on exclusion policies. •Carefully follow group separation and good hygiene procedures.	1 week after illness begins (onset of jaundice or yellow appearance).
Influenza	In the absence of an epidemic, influenza is difficult to diagnose and usually the diagnosis comes after the end of the infectious period, so exclusion will be impractical.	N/A
Measles	•Temporarily exclude the sick child from the child care setting. •Immediately notify your Health Department. •Identify unimmunized children and adults and make sure they get vaccinated and/or exclude them from the child care setting until 2 weeks after rash appears in the last child who had measles in the child care setting.	5 days after rash appears and Health Department says it is safe.
Mumps	•Temporarily exclude the sick child from the child care setting. •Carefully follow group separation and good hygiene practices. •Notify Health Department.	9 days after swelling begins.
Pertussis (Whooping Cough)	•Temporarily exclude the sick child from the child care setting. •Immediately notify your Health Department. •Exclude, until diagnosed by a physician, any child who develops a cough within 2 weeks of the case. arefully follow group separation and good hygiene procedures.	5 days after antibiotics are begun and Health Department says it is safe.
Pinworms	•Temporarily exclude the child from child care setting. •Notify parents.	24 hours after treatment and bathing.

Disease	If a Child in Your Care Has Been Diagnosed With This Disease You Should	When to Allow Child to Return

Pneumonia	•A child diagnosed with this disease will probably be hospitalized. Contact your Health Department and ask what preventive measures to take.
	   —The Health Department may tell you to contact all parents and tell them
	      (1) that their children may have been exposed to a serious contagious disease,
	      (2) that their children should immediately see a physician if they develop *fever, headache, symptoms of infection, or behavior that seems unusual,* and
	      (3) about any additional preventive measures the Health Department has recommended.
	•Carefully follow group separation and good hygiene procedures.
	IMPORTANT: *H-flu* is not the same germ as "flu" or influenza. *H-flu* can cause SERIOUS ILLNESS in young children. If a case of *H-flu* occurs in your facility, TAKE ALL ACTIONS ABOVE.
		Not due to *H-flu*: When treating physician tells you it is safe.
		
		Due to *H-flu*: When the Health Department tells you it is safe.

Ringworm	•Temporarily exclude the child if the lesion cannot be covered.	If unable to cover lesion, after treatment begins and the lesion starts to shrink.
Rubella (German or 3-day measles)	•Temporarily exclude the child from the child care setting. •Immediately notify your Health Department. •Advise any pregnant women in the facility who are not known to be immune to see their physicians. •Carefully follow group separation and good hygiene procedures.	6 days after rash appears and Health Department says it is safe.
Scabies	•Temporarily exclude the child from the child care setting. •You may contact your Health Department for advice about identifying and treating exposed children and adults.	24 hours after treatment has begun.
Streptococcal sore throat (Strep throat)	•Temporarily exclude the child from the child care setting. •Contact your Health Department if 2 or more children are diagnosed with strep throat.	24 hours after antibiotics are begun.
Active Tuberculosis (See Fact Sheet on Tuberculosis for information on nonactive TB infection.)	•Immediately notify your Health Department. •Children with TB may usually remain in child care after treatment as long as they are receiving appropriate treatment.	When Health Department says it is safe.

Note: The term "adult" is used to refer to any adult in the facility (center or home) who may have come in contact with a sick child. This may include more that just those adults actually providing child care. In a home situation, for example, it may also include household occupants.

EMERGENCY ILLNESS AND INJURY PROCEDURES

When parents enroll their child, they should provide you with the contact information and consent that you will need if there is an emergency involving that child. A sample "Child Care Emergency Contact Information and Consent Form" is included in this section. The form includes a statement of parental consent for you to administer first aid and get emergency services for their child. You should request that parents update this form at least once every year.

All parents of children in your care should know your emergency procedures. Let parents know that you are trained in first aid and CPR as taught by the American Red Cross or any other nationally approved first aid training facility. Tell parents how often you take refresher courses. Tell them that in the event of an emergency, you will:

(1) quickly assess the child's health,

(2) call 911 or other appropriate emergency help as needed,

(3) give first aid and CPR, if necessary, and

(4) then contact them or the person they have listed to call in an emergency.

At all times, you should:

- Have emergency numbers posted by the phone--police, ambulance (911), and poison control center. (A list of regional poison control centers is included in this handbook as Appendix 2.)
- Keep parents' consent forms for emergency treatment and numbers for emergency contacts on file. (See sample on next page.)
- Take pediatric CPR and first aid training every year to maintain your American Red Cross certification.
- Post first aid procedures where they can be easily seen. You may want to copy and laminate the list of first aid measures included in this chapter.
- Write up an emergency procedure and evacuation route and make sure you are familiar with it.

24

CHILD CARE EMERGENCY CONTACT INFORMATION AND CONSENT FORM

Child's Name:_____ Birth date: _____

Parent/Guardian #1 Name: _____
    Telephone: Home_____ Work_____ Beeper/Car_____
Parent/Guardian #2 Name:_____
    Telephone: Home_____ Work_____ Beeper/Car_____

EMERGENCY CONTACTS (to whom child may be released if guardian is unavailable)

Name #1:_____Relationship_____
    Telephone: Home_____ Work_____ Beeper/Car_____
Name #2:_____Relationship_____
    Telephone: Home_____ Work_____ Beeper/Car_____

CHILD'S PREFERRED SOURCES OF MEDICAL CARE

    Physician's Name:_____
    Address:_____Telephone:_____

    Dentist's Name:_____
    Address:_____Telephone:_____

    Hospital Name:_____
    Address:_____Telephone_____

    Ambulance Service:_____
    Telephone:_____
    (Parents are responsible for all emergency transportation charges.)

CHILD'S HEALTH INSURANCE

    Insurance Plan:_____ ID#_____
    Subscriber's Name (on insurance card):_____

SPECIAL CONDITIONS, DISABILITIES, ALLERGIES, OR MEDICAL EMERGENCY INFORMATION
_____

PARENT/GUARDIAN CONSENT AND AGREEMENT FOR EMERGENCIES
    As parent/guardian, I consent to have my child receive first aid by facility staff and, if necessary, be transported to receive emergency care. I will be responsible for all charges not covered by insurance. I give consent for the emergency contact person listed above TO ACT ON MY BEHALF until I am available. I agree to review and update this information whenever a change occurs and at least every 6 months.

    Parent/Guardian Signature_____ Date_____
    Parent/Guardian Signature_____ Date_____

- Keep a fully stocked first aid kit in easy reach of all providers, but out of reach of children. Check the first aid kit regularly and restock it as necessary. (See box for what your kit should contain.)

- In addition to the supplies listed for your first aid kit, you should also keep ice cubes or ice bags in the freezer to use to reduce swelling of some injuries.

- Place a stocked first aid kit in every vehicle used to transport the children. In addition to the items in your facility first aid kit, your vehicle kit should also include a bottle of water, soap, coins for a pay telephone, and a first aid guide.

- Don't use first aid sprays and ointments. They may cause allergic reactions or skin damage. Use alcohol or antiseptic wipes.

- Wear gloves if you might come in contact with blood.

What Your First Aid Kit Should Include

- Box of nonporous disposable gloves
- Sealed packages of alcohol wipes or antiseptic wipes
- Small Scissors
- Tweezers (for removing splinters)
- Thermometer
- Adhesive bandage tape
- Sterile gauze squares (2" and 3")
- Triangular bandages
- Flexible roller gauze (1" and 2" widths)
- Triangular bandages
- Safety pins
- Eye dressing
- Insect sting preparation
- Pencil and notepad
- Syrup of ipecac
- Cold pack
- Small splints
- Sealable plastic bags for soiled materials

- Have first aid supplies handy on the playground by keeping a zip-lock plastic bag stocked with disposable gloves, sterile wipes, gauze wrap, and bandaids in your pocket.

26

If an injury occurs:

1. Stay calm.

2. Check for life-threatening situations (choking, severe bleeding, or shock). Do not move a seriously injured child.

3. Call 911 or your local emergency number if the child is seriously hurt.

4. Give CPR or first aid, if necessary.

5. Contact the parent/emergency contact.

6. Record all injuries on a standard form developed for that purpose. At right is an example of a standard injury report form. You may want to list on the back of the form the names of **all of those who witnessed the injury.**

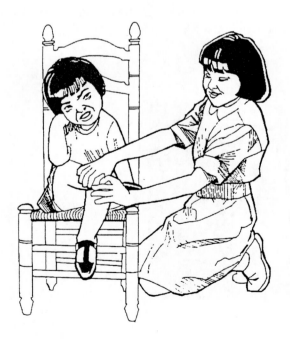

INJURY REPORT FORM

Date of Injury: _____
Time of Injury: _____ ☐am ☐pm
Name of Injured_____
    Sex: ☐Male ☐Female
    Age: ___ years

Where injury happened: _____
_____
How injury happened: _____
_____
_____
_____

Part of body injured: _____
Objects involved (if any): _____
What was done to help the injured: _____
_____
_____

Parent/Guardian advised:
    of injury: ☐yes ☐no
    to seek medical attention: ☐yes ☐no

Supervisor (at time of injury):_____
Person completing form: _____
Date form completed: _____

First Aid Measures

Note: Wear disposable gloves if coming in contact with blood.
Dispose of gloves in a sturdy leakproof plastic bag. Wash hands.

Condition	Action
Abdominal Pain (Severe)	Notify parents. If the child has been injured and has severe or bloody vomiting and is very pale, call 911. Do not allow child to eat or drink.
Abrasions (Scrapes)	Wash abrasion with soap and water. Allow to dry. Cover with a sterile nonstick bandaid or dressing. Notify parents.
Asphyxiation (Suffocation)	**Call 911.** If the child is in a closed area filled with toxic fumes, move the child outside into fresh air. Perform CPR if child is not breathing.
Asthma Attack	**Give prescribed medication**, if any, as previously agreed to by parents. If attack does not stop after the child is given the medication, and the child is still having difficulty breathing, **call 911. If you have no medication** and the attack does not subside within a few minutes, call the parents and ask them to come immediately and take the child for medical care. If the child has difficulty breathing, **call 911.**
Bites and Stings	
<u>Animal:</u>	Wash the wound with soap and water. Notify parents to pick up the child and seek medical advice. If bite is from a bat, fox, raccoon, skunk, or unprovoked cat or dog, or any animal that may have rabies, call the health department, which will contact animal control to catch the animal and observe it for rabies. Do not try to capture the animal yourself. Make note of description of the animal and any identifying characteristics (e.g.,whether dog or cat had a collar).
<u>Human:</u>	Wash the wound with soap and water. Notify parents. If bite causes bleeding, contact the health department for advice.
<u>Insect:</u>	Do not pull out stinger as it may break off; remove the stinger by scraping it out with a fingernail or credit card, then apply a cold cloth. Notify parents. **Call 911** if hives, paleness, weakness, nausea, vomiting, difficult breathing, or collapse occurs.
<u>Snake:</u>	Call local poison control center. Do not apply ice. Notify parents immediately, then the health department. If the child has difficulty breathing, **call 911.**
<u>Ticks:</u>	Notify parents to seek preferences. If parents approve, try to remove tick with tweezers.
<u>Waterlife:</u>	For stingray or catfish stings, submerge affected area in warm water to deactivate the toxin. For other stings, such as from jellyfish, rinse with clean water. Call parents to seek medical care.

28

First Aid Measures

Note: Wear disposable gloves if coming in contact with blood.
Dispose of gloves in a sturdy leakproof plastic bag. Wash hands.

Condition	Action
Bleeding	
External:	For small wounds, apply direct pressure with a gauze pad for 10-15 minutes. (Use gloves.) If bleeding continues or is serious, apply a large pressure dressing and **call 911** immediately.
Internal:	If child has been injured and vomits a large amount of blood or passes blood through the rectum, **call 911.** Otherwise, contact parents to seek medical care. If a child is a hemophiliac and has injured a joint through a minor bump or fall, call the parents. The child may need an injection of blood factor.
Bruises	Apply cold compresses to fresh bruises for the first 15 to 30 minutes. **Note: A child with bruises in unusual locations should be evaluated for child abuse.**
Burns and Scalds	
No blisters:	Place burned extremity in cold water or cover burned area with cold, wet cloths until pain stops (at least 15 minutes).
With blisters:	Same as for no blisters. Do not break blisters. Call parents to take child to get medical care.
Deep, extensive burns:	**Call 911.** Do not apply cold water. Cover child with a clean sheet and then a blanket to keep the child warm.
Electrical:	If possible, disconnect power by shutting off wall switch, throwing a breaker in the electrical box, or any other safe way. Do not directly touch child if power is still on. Use wood or thick dry cloth (nonconducting material) to pull child from power source. **Call 911.** Start CPR if necessary. Notify parents. **Note: A child with burns and scalds should be evaluated for child abuse.**
Croup and Epiglottitis	
Croup:	Call parents to pick up child and get medical care.
Epiglottitis:	**(Similar to croup, but with high fever, severe sore throat, drooling, and difficulty breathing):** Transport child in upright position to medical care. **Call 911** for ambulance if child has severe breathing difficulty.

First Aid Measures

**Note: Wear disposable gloves if coming in contact with blood.
Dispose of gloves in a sturdy leakproof plastic bag. Wash hands.**

Condition	Action
Dental Injuries	
Braces (Broken)	Remove appliance, if it can be done easily. If not, cover sharp or protruding portion with cotton balls, gauze, or chewing gum. If a wire is stuck in gums, cheek, or tongue, DO NOT remove it. Call parent to pick up and take the child to the orthodontist immediately. If the appliance is not injuring the child, no immediate emergency attention is needed.
Cheek, Lip, Tongue (Cut/ Bitten)	Apply ice to bruised areas. If bleeding, apply firm but gentle pressure with a clean gauze or cloth. If bleeding continues after 15 minutes, call the parent to pick up the child and get medical care.
Jaw Injury	Immobilize jaw by having child bite teeth together. Wrap a towel, necktie, or handkerchief around child's head under the chin. Call parent to pick up and take the child to the emergency room.
Tooth (Broken)	Rinse dirt from the injured area with warm water. Place cold compresses over the face in the area of the injury. Locate and save any tooth fragments. Call the parent to pick up and take the child and tooth fragments to the dentist IMMEDIATELY.
Tooth (Knocked Out)	Find the tooth. Handle tooth by the smooth, white portion (crown), not by the root. Rinse the tooth with water, but DO NOT clean it. Place tooth in a cup of milk or water. Call the parent to pick up and take the child and tooth to the dentist IMMEDIATELY. (Time is critical.)
Tooth (Bleeding Due to Loss of Baby Tooth)	Fold and pack clean gauze or cloth over bleeding area. Have child bite on gauze for 15 minutes. Repeat again. If bleeding persists, call parent to pick up and take the child to the dentist.
Sores (Cold/ Canker)	Tell parent and request physician examination if sore persists for more than a week.

First Aid Measures

Note: Wear disposable gloves if coming in contact with blood. Dispose of gloves in a sturdy leakproof plastic bag. Wash hands.

Condition	Action
Eye Injuries	If a chemical is splashed in the eye, immediately flush eye with tepid water, with the eyelid held open. Then remove contact lens, if present, and rinse eye with tepid water for at least 15 minutes. Do not press on injured eye. Gently bandage both eyes shut to reduce eye movement. Call parent to pick up and take child to get medical care.
Fractures **Arm, Leg, Hand, Foot, Fingers, Toes**	Do not move injured part if swollen, broken, or painful. Call parent to pick up and take child to get medical care.
Neck or Back	Do not move child; keep child still. **Call 911** for ambulance.
Frostbite/Freezing	Warm arm, leg, hand, foot, fingers, or toes by holding them in your armpit. Warm ears and noses with a warm palm. For deeper freezing, hold extremity in warm water (105°-110° F) for 20 minutes. Protect involved area from further damage. Apply a sterile gauze and elevate injured area for 40 minutes. Call parents to pick up and take child to get medical care. If child is lethargic, **call 911.**
Frozen to Metal	Do not allow child to pull away from metal. Blow hot breath onto the stuck area or pour **warm** (not hot) water onto the object. Gently release child. If bleeding occurs, such as on the tongue, grasp tongue with folded sterile gauze and apply direct pressure. Call parents to pick up and take child to get medical care.
Head Injuries	Keep child lying down. Call parents **Call 911** if the child is: • complaining of severe or persistent headache • less than 1 year old • oozing blood or fluid from ears or nose • twitching or convulsing • unable to move any body part • unconscious or drowsy • vomiting
Nosebleeds	Have child sit up and lean forward. Loosen tight clothing around neck. Pinch lower end of nose close to nostrils (not on bony part of nose).

First Aid Measures

**Note: Wear disposable gloves if coming in contact with blood.
Dispose of gloves in a sturdy leakproof plastic bag. Wash hands.**

Condition	Action
Poisons	**Immediately, BEFORE YOU DO ANYTHING, call the local poison control center, hospital emergency room, or physician.** (A list of regional poison control centers is included as Appendix 2.) Call parents.

If child needs to go to for medical evaluation, bring samples of what was ingested. Bring with you all containers, labels, boxes, and package inserts that came with the material that the child took in. Look carefully for extra containers around the immediate area where the incident occurred. Try to estimate the total amount of material the child might have taken in, and whether the material was swallowed. inhaled, injected, or spilled in the eyes or on the skin. If possible, also bring with you the child's health file, including consent forms and names and telephone numbers of parents/guardians.

Do not make a child vomit if:
- the child is unconscious or sleepy,
- the child has swallowed a corrosive product (acid/drain cleaner/oven cleaner), or
- the child has swallowed a petroleum product (furniture polish/kerosene/gasoline).

If instructed by the poison control center to make the child vomit:
- Use ipecac syrup:
  Children 1 year to 10 years old:
  1 tablespoon or 3 teaspoons of ipecac and 4 to 8 ounces of water
  Children over 10 years old:
  2 tablespoons of ipecac and 4 to 8 ounces of water
- Follow with another 4 to 8 ounces of water.
- Repeat dose ONCE if child has not vomited in 20 minutes.

If a chemical is spilled on someone, dilute it with water and remove any contaminated clothing. using gloves if possible. Place all contaminated clothing and other items in an airtight bag and label the bag. If the chemical has been splashed int he eye, flush immediately with tepid water and follow instructions listed above for "Eye Injuries."

Some poisons have delayed effects, causing moderate or severe illness many hours or even some days after the child takes the poison. Ask whether the child will need to be observed afterward and for how long. Make sure the child's parents/guardians understand the instructions.

Seizures	Remain calm.

Protect child from injury.
Lie child on his or her side with the head lower than the hips, or on his or her stomach.
Loosen clothing.
Do not put anything in the child's mouth.
Call 911 if seizure lasts more than 5 minutes or if they are the result of a head injury.
Notify parents.

CHILDREN WITH SPECIAL NEEDS

The Americans With Disabilities Act requires that reasonable accommodation should be given to people with disabilities. The law covers children with disabilities seeking reasonable accommodation in a child care setting. In addition to making physical changes, such as installing ramps, wide doors, and rest rooms that can accommodate children in wheel chairs, you may need to provide for a child's special physical, emotional, or psychological needs. Other special needs may include assistance in feeding, following special dietary requirements, giving medicines and/or performing medical procedures, and ensuring that special equipment operates or is used properly.

Before you admit a child with developmental disabilities, you should be sure that the child, you, and any other child care providers who care for the developmentally disabled child is vaccinated against hepatitis B.

You should also be sure that you can comfortably answer the following questions:
1) Does the child's disability require more care than you are reasonably able to provide?
2) Do you have the skills and abilities needed to do medical or other duties required for the child's care, or can you readily get those skills?
3) Is your facility equipped to meet the health and safety needs of this child?
4) Is the extra time you will need to devote to taking care of this child more than you can handle without putting the other children in your care at increased risk for illness or injury or without causing you to neglect their needs?

In deciding whether to admit a child with special needs, you should meet with the child's parents and health care providers to discuss the particular needs of the child. They should tell you the special requirements you will need to meet and specific procedures you will need to do. They should be able to give you an idea of how much of your time the child's special needs will take. The parents or the health care professionals should be able to train you to do the required medical procedures. They should also give you written instructions for procedures, schedules for giving medicines, and menus to meet any eating requirements. If your facility has several groups of children, the special needs child may need special placement within your facility. For example, you may need to place the child within a group of children at a particular developmental level. The child's health care professionals should help you in this and other decisions, and they should serve as ongoing consultants whom you can call for advice. Holding periodic meetings with the parents and the health care professionals to talk about problems, ask questions, and generally review the child's progress helps to make sure that the child's special needs are being met.

The Americans with Disabilities Act requires that every effort to reasonably accommodate the disabled be made. In most cases, such accommodation is compatible with a safe and healthy environment in which all the children in the child care facility can thrive. As a provider responsible for all the children in your care, you should ensure that the extra demands on your time to care for a child with special needs is supported with additional resources, including help from experts, as needed. You should work with the child's parents and health care professionals to make sure that you have the support you need.

MEDICATION ADMINISTRATION

Some children in your child care facility may need to take medications during the hours you provide care for them. Before agreeing to give any medication, whether prescription or over-the-counter, you should obtain written permission from the parent. Also, check with your local child care licensing agency regarding local regulations on administering medications.

You should make sure that any prescribed medication that you give to a child:
- Has the first and last name of the child on the container.
- Has been prescribed by a licensed health professional. Check to see that the name and phone number of the health professional who ordered the medication is on the container.
- Is in the original package or container.
- Has the date the prescription was filled.
- Has an expiration date.
- Has specific instructions for giving, storing, and disposing of the medication.
- Is in a child-proof container.

You may want to suggest to parents that they ask their pharmacist to divide medications into two bottles, one to be kept at home and one to be kept at the child care facility. Children will be less likely to miss a dose of their prescription due to parents forgetting to bring medications to the facility or to take them home at night.

A child's parent may ask that you give a child an over-the-counter medication, such as acetaminophen (Tylenol and other brand names). Over-the-counter medication for each child should be labeled with:
- The child's first and last names.
- The current date.
- The expiration date.
- Specific instructions for giving, storing, and disposing of the medication.
- Name of the health care provider who recommended the medication.

If the child is under 2 years of age, check your state licensing regulations. Some states do not allow a provider to administer over-the-counter medications for children under 2 years of age.

If a child is mistakenly given another child's medication, call the poison control center immediately and follow the advice given. Then call the physician and parents of the child who mistakenly received the medication. **All medications should have childproof caps and be stored out of reach of children. Medications requiring refrigeration should be clearly marked and separated from food.** You may want to keep all medications in a separate, covered container marked "Medications" within the refrigerator.

All medications brought into a child care setting should have child-proof caps and be stored
- in an orderly manner,
- at the proper temperature,
- away from food, and
- out of the reach of children.

Never use medications after the expiration date. Also, do not allow parents to add medications to bottles of formula or milk brought from home. This can lead to inadvertent overdoses.

You should keep a medication record in your child care facility. The record should list:
- The child's name.
- The name of the medication and how and when it is to be given.
- The parent's signature of consent.

You should also keep a log of when you give medications. Each time you give a child a medication, you should list the date, the time, the child's name, the name of the medication, and the dosage given. If more than one provider in your facility gives medicines, each provider should initial the entry, showing that she or he gave the child the medicine. A sample medication log might look like the one below.

MEDICATION LOG					
Date	Time	Child's Name	Name of Medication	Dose Given	Initials

NUTRITION AND FOODS BROUGHT FROM HOME

Eating nutritious food and learning good meal-time behaviors are important for children due to the rapid growth and the major developmental changes that they undergo. Meal times can also be an opportunity for learning and developing social and motor skills, and for being introduced to new foods. Skills such as handwashing, table manners, and carrying on a conversation at the dinner table can be developed and reinforced. Age-appropriate motor skills can be fostered by encouraging children to use child-sized utensils and encouraging children to clear their dishes and utensils from the table. Child-sized furniture and handwashing sinks help children feel comfortable and help the children learn.

To *promote good nutrition*:
- Provide attractive, nourishing food that is appropriate to the children's age and based on a planned, written menu. Contact your local health department or USDA extension service to get the federal guidelines for meals and snacks developed by the U.S. Department of Agriculture's Child Care Food Program and published in the *Code of Federal Regulations*.

Infants
- *Make sure that parents clearly label each child's bottle of formula or breast milk with the child's name and the date. Only use a bottle labeled for that child on that date.* Never accept an unlabeled bottle from a parent. Do not use any unlabeled bottles that have been accidentally accepted. By observing this rule, you can prevent giving a child another child's bottle. However, in the event that a child has mistakenly been given another child's bottle of expressed breastmilk, follow the guidelines under the section on expressed breast milk and possible HIV exposure on the next page.
- Feed infants expressed breast milk or iron-fortified formula on demand unless the parent provides written instructions otherwise.
- Thaw frozen expressed breast milk in the refrigerator or under cold running water.
- Heat bottles in a pan of hot (not boiling) water for 5 minutes, then shake the bottle and test the fluid's temperature before feeding the child. Never heat a child's bottle of formula or expressed breast milk in a microwave. Bottles warmed in microwave ovens heat unevenly and, even after shaking, may have hot spots that could severely burn a child's mouth. Instead, heat a bowl of water in the microwave, then warm the bottle in the bowl of hot water. Or, use a crockpot to heat water for warming bottles.
- Don't allow bottles to warm at room temperature or for long periods: this promotes bacterial growth.
- Always hold young infants during bottle feeding. An infant fed with a propped up bottle is at risk for choking, tooth decay, and ear infections.
- Place older infants in a sitting position for feeding.
- Clean and disinfect reusable bottles, bottle caps, and bottle nipples by washing in a dishwasher or by boiling for 5 minutes just prior to filling.

Toddlers and Preschoolers
- Serve children in care for 8 hours or less *at least one meal and two snacks* or *two meals and one snack.* Offer children in care for more than 8 hours *two meals and two snacks* or *one meal and three snacks.*
- Don't feed children sticky, high sugar foods such as raisins. Foods that stick to the teeth for long periods of time cause tooth decay.
- Don't feed children juice "drinks." Feed them 100 percent juice to get the most nutrition.
- Do not allow children who can walk to carry bottles.
- Don't feed children foods or pieces of food that are the size and shape of a marble. Food this size can be swallowed whole and could become lodged in a child's throat and cause the child to choke. Examples include round slices of hot dogs, whole grapes, marshmallows, chips, and pretzels. Cut round objects, such as grapes, melon balls, or marshmallows, in half. Slice hot dogs lengthwise into quarters and then slice across into pieces. You should not give hard candy, dried fruit, popcorn, and other foods that can't be cut into smaller pieces to young children.

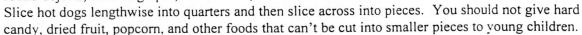

All Children
- Make sure that all children and staff wash their hands both before and after eating.
- Serve food "family style" and eat as a group. This gives the provider the opportunity to promote good table manners by setting an example and gives the children the chance to follow that behavior and talk with the other children.
- Serve small portions, but offer additional servings to meet individual needs.
- Don't force a child to eat. Young children vary the amount of food they consume from day to day and may also have very strong likes and dislikes.
- Don't use food as a reward or punishment.
- Make sure that children with special needs receive any particular foods or assistance in eating that they may require. Check with the child's parents or health care professional for specific instructions.

Expressed Breast Milk and Possible HIV Exposure

If a child has been mistakenly fed another child's bottle of expressed breast milk, the possible exposure to HIV should be treated the same as accidental exposure to other body fluids. You should:

- Inform the parents of the child who was given the wrong bottle that:
    - --their child was given another child's bottle of expressed breast milk,
    - --the risk of transmission of HIV is very small (see discussion below),
    - --they should notify the child's physician of the exposure, and
    - --the child should have a baseline test for HIV.

- Inform the mother who expressed the breast milk of the bottle switch, and ask:
    - --if she has ever had an HIV test and, if so, if she would be willing to share the results with the parents,
    - --if she does not know if she has ever had an HIV test, if she would be willing to contact her obstetrician and find out and, if she has, share the results with the parents,
    - --if she has never had an HIV test, if she would be willing to have one and share the results with

with the parents, and

--when the breast milk was expressed and how it was handled prior to being brought to the facility.

- Provide the exposed child's physician information on when the milk was expressed and how the milk was handled prior to being brought to the facility.

Risk of HIV transmission from expressed breast milk drunk by another child is believed to be low because:

- In the United States, women who are HIV positive and aware of that fact are advised not to breast feed their infants.
- Chemicals present in breast milk act, together with time and cold temperatures, to destroy the HIV present in expressed breast milk.

The risk to child care providers who feed children bottles of expressed breast milk is extremely low because the risk of transmission from skin/mucous membrane exposures to HIV is extremely low (probably much lower than the 0.3% involved with blood and other body fluids with higher levels of virus). Therefore, you do not need to wear gloves when giving bottles of expressed breast milk. If breast milk is spilled on your skin, wash the area with soap and water as soon as possible.

Foods Brought from Home

You should develop a written policy about food brought from home. Parents should be given a copy of this policy when they enroll their child in your child care facility. Foodborne illness and poisoning can result from food that is improperly prepared or stored. You can ensure that the food the children in your care eat is nutritious and safe by planning menus and buying and making the food yourself. Many child care providers provide two snacks and one meal a day to the children in their care. (See sections on Foodborne Illnesses and Nutrition.)

However, if parents provide the food their child is to eat each day, you should make sure that:
- Each individual child's lunch brought from home is clearly labeled with the child's name, the date, and the type of food.
- The food is stored at an appropriate temperature until eaten.
- The food brought from one child's home is not fed to another child.
- Children do not share their food.
- Food brought from home meets the child's nutritional requirements. If you notice that the meal provided by the parents for a child is not nutritionally complete, you should supplement it with food you have on hand. If the food provided for a child consistently does not meet the nutritional requirements of the child, you will need to explain to the parents what foods they need to provide for their child. You can also refer them to their health care professional for nutrition information and meal planning advice.

Sometimes, particularly for birthdays or other special occasions, parents may want to bring a food treat, such as a cake, cupcakes, or other "party" food, to share with all the children at your facility. Tell the parents that food brought into the child-

38

care setting to celebrate these special occasions should be bought at a store or restaurant approved and inspected by the local health authority. Many institutional outbreaks of gastrointestinal illness, including infectious hepatitis, have been linked to eating home-prepared foods. Tell parents that your policy will protect all the children in your care from such foodborne illnesses.

NO SMOKING OR USE OF ALCOHOL OR ILLEGAL DRUGS

You should have a written policy stating that smoking tobacco (smoking cigars, cigarettes, or pipes) and using or having illegal drugs are prohibited in your facility at all times and alcohol use is prohibited when children are in care. Discuss this policy with parents and inform them of the dangers of these substances to children.

No children should be exposed to cigarette smoke. Inhaling secondhand cigarette smoke has been linked to respiratory problems in children. These children are at increased risk of developing bronchitis, pneumonia, and otitis media when they get common respiratory infections such as colds. Children with asthma are especially in danger of having their conditions get worse when they are exposed to cigarette smoke. Smoking in rooms other than those which the children occupy is not a sufficient remedy. Smoke gets into the ventilation system and is distributed throughout the building. Therefore, no smoking should be allowed at any time in any home or building that children occupy.

FOLLOWING PROTECTIVE PRACTICES
TO REDUCE DISEASE AND INJURY

By adopting some basic disease and injury prevention practices and procedures, you can make the child care environment safer and healthier. This chapter addresses ways to reduce stress in the child care environment; the number and ages of children who can reasonably be cared for by each provider; proper hand washing, diapering, and cleaning and disinfection procedures; and food preparation and serving practices.

REDUCING BACK INJURY AMONG PROVIDERS

Back injury is the most common cause of occupational injury for child care providers. You can prevent back injury by using:

- Proper lifting technique, such as keeping the child as close as possible to you and avoiding any twisting motion as you lift the child. Also, always lower the crib side before lifting the child out.
- Adult furniture; providers should not use child-sized chairs, tables, or desks.
- Adult-height changing tables.
- A ramp or small, stable stepladders or stairs to allow children, with constant supervision, to climb up to changing tables or other places to which they would ordinarily be lifted.
- Convenient equipment for moving children, reducing the necessity for carrying them long distances. For example, using a multi-seat carriage to transport children to a nearby park.
- Comfortable chairs with back support (rockers, gliders, etc.) for holding children for long periods of time.

STRESS REDUCTION AMONG PROVIDERS

Stress among child care providers is an important problem because it not only affects the provider's health, but also the quality of care that the provider is able to give. A provider who is under too much stress will not be able to offer the praise, nurturing, and direction that children need for good development.

Sources of occupational stress for providers may include:
- Tension between parents and care givers.
- Too much work to do in too little time.
- Feeling unable to make full use of their skills and abilities.
- Too many children per provider to allow the provider to sufficiently tend to the children's individual needs.
- Noise.
- Immediacy of the needs of the children.

For those providers who work in child care centers, stress may also be a result of:
- Not fully understanding what is expected on the job or how to perform it.
- Poor relationships with coworkers.
- Having little control over how their jobs are performed.
- Having few or no opportunities for career advancement.
- Lack of clear communication with supervisors.

If you work in your own family child care home, you can reduce stress by making and following clear work policies and procedures, and by getting training in those areas of your work that you are not comfortable in performing. If you are responsible for managing other providers:

- Explain your center's work procedures to the staff, giving them an opportunity to ask questions and have them answered. Make sure they clearly understand your policies regarding guidance and discipline of children or managing children's behavior.
- Include in your policies and procedures clear direction on how to deal with conflicts with parents regarding child care.
- Be available to help providers when they need you and give them the resources they need to do their work well.
- Give providers "ownership" in their work by making it clear that you want to know what they feel would help them do their jobs better.
- Review the amount and type of work each provider is expected to do and make sure both are reasonable.
- Watch providers performing their jobs. Let them know what they are doing well and what needs to be improved. Offer advice on how to improve.
- Provide training to enhance providers' knowledge and skills.
- Develop a career ladder (e.g., based on training and work responsibilities), when possible, through which providers can advance within your facility.
- Encourage providers to suggest solutions to problems and implement them.
- Encourage good working relationships among all providers. Immediately investigate disagreements to determine the source and find solutions. A solution may be as simple as explaining a procedure.
- Advocate for fair provider salaries.

CHILD-TO-STAFF RATIOS

The child-to-staff ratio (the number of children for which each child care provider is responsible) affects the quality of care a child care provider can give to each child. Small group sizes and low child-to-staff ratios are recommended by the American Public Health Association (APHA), the American Academy of Pediatrics (AAP), and the National Association for the Education of Young Children (NAEYC). Having a smaller number of infants/toddlers/children for each adult to take care of has been associated with:

- Children imitating earlier, and more often than usual, the speech and gestures of others.
- Providers having more time to give the best care to children.
- Children talking and playing more often.
- Children being in distress less often.
- Children being less exposed to danger.

Grouping children in smaller numbers has been associated with:

- Providers being able to give better attention to the children.
- Children having more positive developmental outcomes.
- Children being more cooperative and more responsive to adults and other children.
- Children being more likely to speak without being urged.

- Children being less likely to wander aimlessly or be uninvolved in activities.
- Children scoring higher on standardized tests.

The chart below gives American Public Health Association/American Academy of Pediatrics (APHA/AAP) recommendations by age for group size and child-to-staff ratios. Your state's regulations may be different.

Age	Maximum Group Size	Child-to-Staff Ratio
0 to 24 months	6	3:1
25 to 30 months	8	4:1
31 to 35 months	10	5:1
3 years	14	7:1
4 to 6 years	16	8:1

SUPERVISION

No child should ever be left alone while in child care. You should supervise children at all times, including when children are sleeping and while they are using the bathroom. You should have a written policy regarding supervision and discipline of children. Your policy should describe the type of guidance you will provide to the children, based on their age, and should specify that the following are strictly prohibited: corporal punishment, emotional abuse, humiliation, abusive language, and withdrawal of food and other basic needs. Guidance should include positive, nonviolent, nonabusive methods for achieving discipline. The policy should also include any specific precautions to be taken during play in high-risk areas or while using high-risk equipment. Finally, your policy should state that any acts of aggression by children, such as fighting, biting, or hitting will result in the separation of the children involved; attention to any harmed individual, including medical attention, if necessary; and notification of parents of the children involved. After any incident you should review whether you were giving the children enough supervision and whether the activities in which the children were engaged are appropriate. You may need to change how you supervise the children and the activities you plan for them. Your policy should also state what will happen if such incidents recur.

GROUP SEPARATION OF CHILDREN

In a child care setting, you can reduce the risk of illness and injury by separating older children from younger children and those in diapers from those not in diapers. The presence of infants and toddlers under 3 years old who are still in diapers poses a higher risk for the spread of diarrheal diseases and hepatitis A. Separating groups of children can help to keep infectious diseases of one group from spreading to other groups. Separating children by age also is helpful in encouraging children to participate in activities appropriate to their age.

HANDWASHING

Most experts agree that the single most effective practice that prevents the spread of germs in the child care setting is good handwashing by child care providers, children, and others. Some activities in particular expose children and providers to germs or the opportunity to spread them. You can stop the spread of germs by washing your hands and teaching the children in your care good handwashing practices.

When Hands Should Be Washed

Children:
- Upon arrival at the child care setting.
- Immediately before and after eating.
- After using the toilet or having their diapers changed.
- Before using water tables.
- After playing on the playground.
- After handling pets, pet cages, or other pet objects.
- Whenever hands are visibly dirty.
- Before going home.

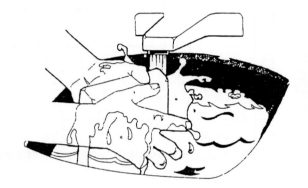

Providers:
- Upon arrival at work.
- Immediately before handling food, preparing bottles, or feeding children.
- After using the toilet, assisting a child in using the toilet, or changing diapers.
- After contacting a child's body fluids, including wet or soiled diapers, runny noses, spit, vomit, etc.
- After handling pets, pet cages, or other pet objects.
- Whenever hands are visibly dirty or after cleaning up a child, the room, bathroom items, or toys.
- After removing gloves used for any purpose.*
- Before giving or applying medication or ointment to a child or self.
- Before going home.

*If gloves are being used, hands should be washed immediately after gloves are removed even if hands are not visibly contaminated. Use of gloves alone will not prevent contamination of hands or spread of germs and should not be considered a substitute for handwashing.

Rubbing hands together under running water is the most important part of washing away infectious germs. Premoistened towelettes or wipes and waterless hand cleaners should not be used as a substitute for washing hands with soap and running water. Towelettes should only be used to remove residue, such as food off a baby's face or feces from a baby's bottom during diaper changing. When running water is unavailable, such as during an outing, towelettes may be used as a temporary measure until hands can be washed under running water. A child care provider may use a towelette to clean hands while diapering a child who cannot be left alone on a changing table that is not within reach of running water. However, hands should be washed as soon as diapering is completed and child is removed from the changing table. Water basins should not be used as an alternative to running water. If forced to use a water basin as a temporary measure, clean and disinfect the basin between each use. Outbreaks have been linked with sharing wash water and washbasins.

How to Wash Hands

- Always use warm, running water and a mild, preferably liquid, soap. Antibacterial soaps may be used, but are not required. Premoistened cleansing towelettes do not effectively clean hands and do not take the place of handwashing.

- Wet the hands and apply a small amount (dime to quarter size) of liquid soap to hands.

- Rub hands together vigorously until a soapy lather appears and continue for at least 15 seconds. Be sure to scrub between fingers, under fingernails, and around the tops and palms of the hands.

- Rinse hands under warm running water. Leave the water running while drying hands.

- Dry hands with a clean, disposable (or single use) towel, being careful to avoid touching the faucet handles or towel holder with clean hands.

- Turn the faucet off using the towel as a barrier between your hands and the faucet handle.

- Discard the used towel in a trash can lined with a fluid-resistant (plastic) bag. Trash cans with foot-pedal operated lids are preferable.

- Consider using hand lotion to prevent chapping of hands. If using lotions, use liquids or tubes that can be squirted so that the hands do not have direct contact with container spout. Direct contact with the spout could contaminate the lotion inside the container.

- When assisting a child in handwashing, either hold the child (if an infant) or have the child stand on a safety step at a height at which the child's hands can hang freely under the running water. Assist the child in performing all of the above steps and then wash your own hands.

DIAPERING

Two different diaper changing methods may be used to minimize the risk of transmitting infection from one child to another or to a provider. One method involves the use of gloves and the other does not. The method you select should be used consistently in your child care setting. Whichever method you choose, you should never wash or rinse diapers or clothes soiled with fecal material in the child care setting. Because of the risk of splashing, and gross contamination of hands, sinks, and bathroom surfaces, rinsing increases the risk that you, other providers, and the children would be exposed to germs that cause infection. All soiled clothing should be bagged and sent home with the child without rinsing. (You may dump solid feces into a toilet.) You need to tell parents about this procedure and why it is important.

The following recommended procedure notes additional steps to be included when using gloves. Gloves are not required, but some people prefer to use gloves to prevent fecal material from getting under their nails. Child care providers should keep their fingernails short, groomed, and clean. Using a soft nail brush to clean under the nails during handwashing will remove soil under the nails. Always maintain a pleasant attitude while changing a child's diaper. Never show disgust or scold a child who has had a loose stool.

Recommended Procedure for Diapering a Child

1. **Organize needed supplies within reach:**
    - •fresh diaper and clean clothes (if necessary)
    - •dampened paper towels or premoistened towelettes for cleaning child's bottom
    - •child's personal, labeled, ointment (if provided by parents)
    - •trash disposal bag

2. **Place a disposable covering (such as roll paper) on the portion of the diapering table where you will place the child's bottom.** Diapering surfaces should be smooth, nonabsorbent, and easy to clean. Don't use areas that come in close contact with children during play, such as couches, floor areas where children play, etc.

3. **If using gloves, put them on now.**

4. **Using only your hands, pick up and hold the child away from your body.** Don't cradle the child in your arms and risk soiling your clothing.

5. **Lay the child on the paper or towel.**

6. **Remove soiled diaper (and soiled clothes).**

7. **Put disposable diapers in a plastic-lined trash receptacle.**

8. **Put soiled reusable diaper and/or soiled clothes WITHOUT RINSING in a plastic bag to give to parents.**

9. **Clean child's bottom with a premoistened disposable towelette or a dampened, single-use, disposable towel.**

10. **Place the soiled towelette or towel in a plastic-lined trash receptacle.**

11. **If the child needs a more thorough washing, use soap, running water, and paper towels.**

12. **Remove the disposable covering from beneath the child. Discard it in a plastic-lined receptacle.**

13. **If you are wearing gloves, remove and dispose of them now in a plastic-lined receptacle.**

14. **Wash your hands. NOTE:** The diapering table should be next to a sink with running water so that you can wash your hands without leaving the diapered child unattended. However, if a sink is not within reach of the diapering table, **don't leave the child unattended on the diapering table** to go to a sink; wipe your hands with a premoistened towelette instead. **NEVER** leave a child alone on the diapering table.

15. **Wash the child's hands under running water.**

16. **Diaper and dress the child.**

17. **Disinfect the diapering surface immediately after you finish diapering the child.** (See section on "Cleaning and Disinfection" later in this chapter.)

18. **Return the child to the activity area.**

19. **Clean and disinfect:**
    - •The diapering area,
    - •all equipment or supplies that were touched, and
    - •soiled crib or cot, if needed.

20. **Wash your hands under running water.**

USING TOILET-TRAINING EQUIPMENT

Potty chairs are difficult to keep clean and out of the reach of children. Small size flushable toilets or modified toilet seats and step aids are preferable. If potty chairs are used for toilet training, you should use potty chairs only in a bathroom area and out of reach of toilets or other potty chairs. After each use of a potty chair, you should:

- Immediately empty the contents into a toilet, being careful not to splash or touch the water in the toilet.
- Rinse the potty with water from a sink used only for custodial cleaning. DO NOT rinse the potty in a sink used for washing hands. A sink used for food preparation should NEVER be used for this purpose.
- Dump the rinse water into a toilet.
- Wash and disinfect the potty chair. (See "Cleaning and Disinfection," below.)
- Wash and disinfect the sink and all exposed surfaces.
- Wash your hands thoroughly.

CLEANING AND DISINFECTION

Keeping the child care environment clean and orderly is very important for health, safety, and the emotional well-being of both children and providers. One of the most important steps in reducing the number of germs, and therefore the spread of disease, is the thorough cleaning of surfaces that could possibly pose a risk to children or staff. Surfaces considered most likely to be contaminated are those with which children are most likely to have close contact. These include toys that children put in their mouths, crib rails, food preparation areas, and surfaces likely to become very contaminated with germs, such as diaper-changing areas.

Routine cleaning with soap and water is the most useful method for removing germs from surfaces in the child care setting. Good mechanical cleaning (scrubbing with soap and water) physically reduces the numbers of germs from the surface, just as handwashing reduces the numbers of germs from the hands. Removing germs in the child care setting is especially important for soiled surfaces which cannot be treated with chemical disinfectants, such as some upholstery fabrics.

However, some items and surfaces should receive an additional step, **disinfection**, to kill germs after cleaning with soap and and rinsing with clear water. Items that can be washed in a dishwasher or hot cycle of a washing machine do not have to be disinfected because these machines use water that is hot enough for a long enough period of time to kill most germs. The disinfection process uses chemicals that are stronger than soap and water. Disinfection also usually requires soaking or drenching the item for several minutes to give the chemical time to kill the remaining germs. Commercial products that meet the Environmental Protection Agency's (EPA's) standards for "hospital grade" germicides (solutions that kill germs) may be used for this purpose. One of the most commonly used chemicals for disinfection in child care settings is a homemade solution of household bleach and water. Bleach is cheap and easy to get. The solution of bleach and water is easy to mix, is nontoxic, is safe if handled properly, and kills most infectious agents. (Be aware that some infectious agents are not killed by bleach. For example, cryptosporidia is only killed by ammonia or hydrogen peroxide.)

A solution of bleach and water loses its strength very quickly and easily. It is weakened by organic material, evaporation, heat, and sunlight. Therefore, bleach solution should be mixed fresh each day to make sure it is effective. Any leftover solution should be discarded at the end of the day. NEVER mix bleach with anything but fresh tap water! Other chemicals may react with bleach and create and release a toxic chlorine gas.

Keep the bleach solution you mix each day in a cool place out of direct sunlight and out of the reach of children. (Although a solution of bleach and water mixed as shown in the accompanying box should not be harmful if accidentally swallowed, you should keep all chemicals away from children.)

If you use a commercial (brand-name) disinfectant, read the label and always follow the manufacturer's instructions exactly.

Recipe for Bleach Disinfecting Solution
(For use in bathrooms, diapering areas, etc.)

1/4 cup bleach
1 gallon of cool water

OR

1 tablespoon bleach
1 quart cool water

Add the household bleach (5.25% sodium hypochlorite) to the water.

Recipe for Weaker
Bleach Disinfecting Solution
(For use on toys, eating utensils, etc.)

1 tablespoon bleach
1 gallon cool water

Add the bleach to the water.

Washing and Disinfecting Toys

- Infants and toddlers should not share toys. Toys that children (particularly infants and toddlers) put in their mouths should be washed and disinfected between uses by individual children. Toys for infants and toddlers should be chosen with this in mind. If you can't wash a toy, it probably is not appropriate for an infant or toddler.

- When an infant or toddler finishes playing with a toy, you should retrieve it from the play area and put it in a bin reserved for dirty toys. This bin should be out of reach of the children. Toys can be washed at a later, more convenient time, and then transferred to a bin for clean toys and safely reused by other children.

- To wash and disinfect a hard plastic toy:
    - Scrub the toy in warm, soapy water. Use a brush to reach into the crevices.
    - Rinse the toy in clean water.
    - Immerse the toy in a mild bleach solution (see above) and allow it to soak in the solution for 10-20 minutes.
    - Remove the toy from the bleach solution and rinse well in cool water.
    - Air dry.

- Hard plastic toys that are washed in a dishwasher or cloth toys washed in the hot water cycle of a washing machine do not need to be additionally disinfected.

- Children in diapers should only have washable toys. Each group of children should have its own toys. Toys should not be shared with other groups.

- Stuffed toys used by only a single child should be cleaned in a washing machine every week, or more frequently if heavily soiled.

- Toys and equipment used by older children and not put into their mouths should be cleaned at least weekly and when obviously soiled. A soap and water wash followed by clear water rinsing and air drying should be adequate. No disinfection is required. (These types of toys and equipment include blocks, dolls, tricycles, trucks, and other similar toys.)

- Do not use wading pools, especially for children in diapers. (See "Outdoor Playground Areas..." for further discussion.)

- Water play tables can spread germs. To prevent this:
    - Disinfect the table with chlorine bleach solution before filling it with water.
    - Disinfect all toys to be used in the table with chlorine bleach solution. Avoid using sponge toys. They can trap bacteria and are difficult to clean.
    - Have all children wash their hands before and after playing in the water table.
    - Do not allow children with open sores or wounds to play in the water table.
    - Carefully supervise the children to make sure they don't drink the water.
    - Discard water after play is over.

Washing and Disinfecting Bathroom and Other Surfaces

Bathroom surfaces , such as faucet handles and toilet seats, should be washed and disinfected several times a day, if possible, but at least once a day or when soiled. The bleach and water solution or chlorine-containing scouring powders or other commercial bathroom surface cleaners/disinfectants can be used in these areas.
Surfaces that infants and young toddlers are likely to touch or mouth, such as crib rails, should be washed with soap and water and disinfected with a nontoxic disinfectant, such as bleach solution, at least once

48

every day, more often if visibly soiled. After the surface has been drenched or soaked with the disinfectant for at least 10 minutes, surfaces likely to be mouthed should be thoroughly wiped with a fresh towel moistened with tap water. Be sure not to use a toxic cleaner on surfaces likely to be mouthed. Floors, low shelves, door knobs, and other surfaces often touched by children wearing diapers should be washed and disinfected at least once a day and whenever soiled.

Washing and Disinfecting Diaper Changing Areas

Diaper changing areas should:
- Only be used for changing diapers.
- Be smooth and nonporous, such as formica (NOT wood).
- Have a raised edge or low "fence" around the area to prevent a child from falling off.
- Be next to a sink with running water.
- Not be used to prepare food, mix formula, or rinse pacifiers.
- Be easily accessible to providers.
- Be out of reach of children.

Diaper changing areas should be cleaned and disinfected after each diaper change as follows:
- Clean the surface with soap and water and rinse with clear water.
- Dry the surface with a paper towel.
- Thoroughly wet the surface with the recommended bleach solution.
- Air dry. Do not wipe.

Washing and Disinfecting Clothing, Linen, and Furnishings

Do not wash or rinse clothing soiled with fecal material in the child care setting. You may empty solid stool into the toilet, but be careful not to splash or touch toilet water with your hands. Put the soiled clothes in a plastic bag and seal the bag to await pick up by the child's parent or guardian at the end of the day. Always wash your hands after handling soiled clothing.

Explain to parents that washing or rinsing soiled diapers and clothing increases the chances that you and the children may be exposed to germs that cause diseases. Although receiving soiled clothes isn't pleasant, remind parents that this policy protects the health of all children and providers. Each item of sleep equipment, including cribs, cots, mattresses, blankets, sheets, etc., should be cleaned and sanitized before being assigned to a specific child. The bedding items should be labeled with that child's name, and should only be used by that child. Children should not share bedding. Infants' linens (sheets, pillowcases, blankets) should be cleaned and sanitized daily, and crib mattresses should be cleaned and sanitized weekly and when soiled or wet. Linens from beds of older children should be laundered at least weekly and whenever soiled. However, if a child inadvertently uses another child's bedding, you should change the linen and mattress cover before allowing the assigned child to use it again. All blankets should be changed and laundered routinely at least once a month.

Cleaning Up Body Fluid Spills

Spills of body fluids, including blood, feces, nasal and eye discharges, saliva, urine, and vomit should be cleaned up immediately. Wear gloves unless the fluid can be easily contained by the material (e.g., paper tissue or cloth) being used to clean it up. Be careful not to get any of the fluid you are cleaning in your eyes, nose, mouth or any open sores you may have. Clean and disinfect any surfaces, such as countertops and floors, on which body fluids have been spilled. Discard fluid-contaminated material in a plastic bag that has been securely sealed. Mops used to clean up body fluids should be (1) cleaned, (2) rinsed with a disinfecting solution, (3) wrung as dry as possible, and (4) hung to dry completely. Be sure to wash your hands after cleaning up any spill.

USING AND HANDLING TOOTHBRUSHES

Toothbrushing is a lifelong preventive habit important to maintain oral health and prevent tooth decay. Toothbrushing in the child care setting helps children to develop this habit. To brush teeth properly and to prevent infections from spreading from germs found in saliva and blood on toothbrushes:

- Always supervise children when they are brushing their teeth.
- Make sure that each child has his/her own toothbrush clearly labeled with his/her name. Do not allow children to share or borrow toothbrushes.
- Apply (or have child apply) a pea-sized amount of fluoride toothpaste to a dry toothbrush.
- Instruct each child to brush his/her teeth and then spit out the toothpaste.
- Using a paper cup, each child should rinse his/her mouth out with water. Dispose of the cup.
- Store each toothbrush so it cannot touch any other toothbrush and allow it to air dry.
- Never "disinfect" toothbrushes. If a child uses another child's toothbrush or if two toothbrushes come in contact, throw them away and give the children new toothbrushes.
- If a child uses the toothbrush of another child that is known to be ill or have a chronic bloodborne infection (such as Hepatitis B or HIV), parents of the child who used the ill child's brush should be notified.
- Replace toothbrushes every 3 to 4 months or sooner if bristles have lost their tone.

FOOD SAFETY AND SANITATION

Poor food preparation, handling, or storage can quickly result in food being contaminated with germs and may lead to illness if the contaminated food is eaten. Contact your local health department to obtain the local regulations and standards for food safety and sanitation and to ask about the availability of a food handler course in your area.

The best way to wash, rinse, and disinfect dishes and eating utensils is to use a dishwasher. If a dishwasher is not available or cannot be installed, a three-compartment sink will be needed to wash, rinse, and disinfect dishes. A two-compartment or one-compartment sink can be used by adding one or two dishpans, as needed. In addition to three compartments or dishpans, you will need a dishrack with a drainboard to allow dishes and utensils to air dry. To wash, rinse, and disinfect dishes by hand:

- Fill one sink compartment or dishpan with hot tap water and a dishwashing detergent.
- Fill the second compartment or dishpan with hot tap water.
- Fill the third compartment or dishpan with hot tap water and 1-1/2 tablespoons of liquid chlorine bleach for each gallon of water.
- Scrape dishes and utensils and dispose of excess food.
- Immerse scraped dish or utensil in first sink compartment or dishpan and wash thoroughly.
- Rinse dish or utensil in second dishpan of clear water.
- Immerse dish or utensil in third dishpan of chlorinated water for at least 1 minute.
- Place dish or utensil in rack to air dry.

Note: Food preparation and dishwashing sinks should only be used for these activities and should never be used for routine handwashing or diaper changing activities.

Information on how to prevent foodborne illnesses by safely handling food. see "Foodborne Illnesses in the Child Care Setting" in the Disease section of this handbook.

MAINTAINING A SAFE AND HEALTHY CHILD CARE FACILITY

SAFETY AND SECURITY PRECAUTIONS

All child care facilities should have a written safety plan that addresses the safety and security of the children and providers. Below are some of the issues your safety plan should include.

Release of Children

To ensure safety and security of the children in your care, you should:

- Maintain a log for signing children in and out of your facility. Note the date, time. child's name, and name of the person dropping off or picking up the child.
- Maintain a file of the names, addresses, and telephone numbers of persons authorized to pick up each child in your care. **You should only release a child to a person for whom you have written consent by the custodial parent.** Never honor a telephone authorization unless there is a prior written consent by the custodial parent on file. Telephone authorization could be falsely provided by a person pretending to be the child's custodial parent.
- Contact your local police department for advice on how to avoid releasing a child into an unsafe situation, such as to a parent who appears to be intoxicated (under the influence of drugs or alcohol). Have a written policy and inform all parents/guardians of it when the child is admitted to your care.

Transport of Children

Traffic accidents or automobile crashes are one of the most common causes of injury and death for children. You should pay particular attention to preventing vehicle injuries.

- Always use an approved car seat for any child under 40 lbs. Continue to use the car seat until the child outgrows it. All other child and adult passengers should use seat belts and harnesses. For more information on national child safety seat requirements, call the National Highway Transportation Safety Administration's Auto Safety Hotline, 1-800-424-9393.
- Only allow a vehicle to be operated by a person with a valid driver's license for that type of vehicle.
- Never allow anyone to operate a vehicle under the influence of alcohol or drugs, including prescription drugs that may make a person drowsy.
- Make sure that any vehicle used to transport children is licensed and registered according to state laws.
- Equip each vehicle with a first aid kit and emergency identification and contact information for all the children being transported.
- Properly maintain each vehicle.
- Air condition a vehicle when the temperature is above 75°F; heat it when the temperature is below 50°F.
- Never allow smoking or playing audio equipment loudly in a vehicle when transporting children. A driver should never use earphones while driving.
- Have enough providers present to make sure that proper child-to-provider ratios are maintained. Do

count the driver as a provider. A driver is not able to properly supervise children while driving.

- Never leave a child unsupervised in a vehicle.
- Carefully supervise children getting in or out of a vehicle to avoid injury. Upon boarding, make sure each child is properly buckled in. Upon exiting, make sure each child is clear of the path of the vehicle and any other traffic.
- Before leaving the vehicle, check to make sure that all children have exited.

EVACUATION PLAN AND DRILLS FOR FIRES, CHEMICAL EMERGENCIES, AND OTHER DISASTERS

Each child care facility should have a written plan for evacuation in the event of fire. The plan should be posted in a visible area. You should also write up procedures for a chemical emergency (spill or accidental release) and make sure you are familiar with your city's (or county's) Community Response Plan, available from your fire department, Local Emergency Planning Committee, or State Emergency Response Commission. Each facility, as appropriate for its geographic area, should also have an evacuation plan for blizzard, earthquake, flood, hurricane, tornado, power failure, or other disasters that could create structural damages to the facility or pose health hazards. You should practice drills for fire (and for tornadoes in areas where they occur) every month. Drills for hurricanes and earthquakes should be practiced every 6 months or annually in areas in which they are likely to occur. Keep a record of your practice drills.

FIRE SAFETY

Smoke detectors should be installed on the ceiling, or 6 to 12 inches below the ceiling, every 40 feet on each floor of your child care facility. The detectors should not be installed above "drop down" ceilings or behind acoustic walls. Test the detectors monthly, and replace batteries at least every year. Install and maintain enough A-B-C-type fire extinguishers to be in accordance with insurance requirements or fire marshall recommendations. Post instructions for their use on or near the extinguishers. Make sure you and anyone else who works with you know how to use the extinguishers.

ELECTRICAL FIXTURES AND OUTLETS

Appliances, electrical wiring, fixtures, and outlets can be a hazard to the safety of children in your care. You should make sure that:

- The electrical service in your facility and installation of any fixtures are certified by an electrical code inspector.
- Electrical outlets within the reach of children are covered with child-resistant covers. Shock stops (safety plugs) should be placed over all unused outlets.
- All electrical cords are out of the reach of children.
- No electrical cords are frayed or overloaded.
- No extension cords are used unless absolutely necessary. If you must use an extension cord, do not place the cord under carpeting or across any area with a water source.
- Fans used to cool an area have 1/4 inch bladeguard openings and are mounted high on the wall or ceiling.

- No portable, open-flame, kerosene space heaters or portable gas stoves are used for heating.
- Electric space heaters are used only as a last alternative for heating. If you must use them, make sure they are Underwriters' Laboratories-approved, not within reach of children, have a protective covering, and are placed on a stable surface at least 3 feet from curtains, papers, and furniture.

STAIRWAYS/STEPS AND WALKWAYS

Stairways, steps, and walkways should be kept in good repair and well lighted. Stairways with three or more steps should have handrails on both sides. Handrails should be securely mounted to the walls or stairs. All freestanding stairs (not between walls), balconies, landings, porches and similar structures must have protective railings. The balusters (upright spokes) of handrails should be less than 3-1/2 inches apart to prevent children from slipping through. The bottom rail should be less than 6 inches above the floor to prevent children from slipping under.

INDOOR FURNISHINGS AND EQUIPMENT

Furnishings, equipment, and materials used in a child care facility should be safe for children. Child-sized furniture or furniture and equipment that has been adapted for children's use helps to prevent falls and other injuries. Items with corners, protruding nails or bolts, loose or rusty parts, small parts that could be swallowed, or with toxic finishes, such as lead-based paint, should not be used. Floors, walls, and ceilings should be smooth, in good repair, and easy to clean. Floors should be free from bare concrete, cracks, dampness, drafts, splinters, sliding carpets, and telephone jacks or electrical outlets. Carpets should be clean, in good repair, and made of nonflammable and nontoxic fibers. Cords from window coverings should not be within reach of children.

OUTDOOR PLAYGROUND AREAS AND EQUIPMENT AND POOLS

Playground injuries are the leading cause of serious injuries at child care facilities. To prevent such injuries, you can take action to make outdoor play safer. Make sure that your outdoor play area is enclosed with a fence or natural barriers (such as a hedge) at least 4 feet high, with the bottom no more than 3 1/2 inches off the ground. A fence should have at least two gates with latches above the reach of small children. The area should be clean and safe with no debris, dilapidated structures, broken or worn equipment, toxic plants, or other objects or materials that could cause injury. If you suspect the soil may contain hazardous levels of chemicals or toxins, have it tested.

As with indoor equipment, outdoor equipment should not have sharp corners, protruding nails or bolts, loose or rusty parts, small parts that could be swallowed, or toxic finishes, such as lead-based paint. Holes or abandoned wells in the area should be filled or sealed. The area should also be well drained, with no standing water. Both sunlit areas and shaded areas should be provided. Climbers and swings should have a resilient surface, such as sand, uniform wood chips, etc., beneath them and within the fall zone that will cushion a child's fall.

Any pools of water (swimming pools, fish ponds, etc.) should be enclosed with a fence at least 5 feet high and no more than 3 1/2 inches off the ground. Inground pools should be surrounded by a 4-foot wide, nonskid surface. The pool should be covered when not in use. The water in pools used for wading or swimming should be maintained between pH 7.2 and pH 8.2. (You can buy a water testing kit at any pool supply store.) Water temperatures should be between 82°F and 93°F.

Small, portable wading pools should not be used. Because they have no filtration system, the stagnant water provides a perfect setting for bacteria to grow. Instead, use sprinklers, hoses, or water tables as an alternative for water play.

SMALL OBJECTS AND TOYS

Small objects and toys with small parts can be a hazard to children. Keep the following out of the reach of children under 4 years of age:
- Coins
- Marbles
- Plastic bags or styrofoam objects
- Rubber balloons
- Safety pins
- Toys, objects. or toys or objects with parts smaller than 1 1/4 inches in diameter and 2 1/4 inches long
- Toys with sharp points and edges

FIREARMS

Firearms, including pellet or BB guns (loaded or unloaded); darts; or cap pistols should not be kept on the premises of any child care facility. These items can cause severe injuries and death. If the child care facility is a family child care home, the personal firearms of the homeowner should be kept unloaded in a locked cabinet in an area of the home away from the child care area and to which the children do not have access.

WATER TEMPERATURES

Hot water heated to at least 120°F is needed in every child care facility to clean, sanitize, and disinfect food utensils and sanitize laundry. However, very hot water (above 120°F) can be a hazard to children. Tap water burns are a leading cause of nonfatal burns. Children under 5 years of age are the most frequent victims of such burns. Water heated to 130°F takes only 30 seconds to burn the skin. If the water is heated to 120°F, only 10°F cooler, it takes 2 minutes to burn the skin. That extra 2 minutes could be enough to get a child away from the hot water source and avoid a burn.

Such scalds can be prevented by "scald resistant" faucets, which have built-in temperature valves. The thermostat for the valve can be set between a range of degrees. Some states require scald-resistant faucets in all new construction. You should have scald-resistant faucets installed in those sinks or bathing fixtures that children use. You may need to have a plumbing contractor install these faucets. Have the contractor set the valve at or below 120°F.

As mentioned earlier in the discussion of outdoor playground equipment, the water in pools used for wading or swimming should be maintained between 82°F and 93°F.

CHEMICAL TOXINS

Children in child care and child care providers have many opportunities for exposure to toxic chemicals and substances. Cleaning products, pesticides, arts and crafts supplies, common household products, and even household plants can be hazardous. You can be exposed to toxic substances by breathing them in (inhaling), swallowing (ingesting) them, or getting them in your eyes or on your skin.

One type of exposure is through breathing in toxic fumes. Breathing toxic substances can damage the respiratory system. Once in the lungs, toxins can then be absorbed into the bloodstream. From the bloodstream, toxins may be deposited in the organs, where they can cause damage. Reactions to breathing toxins occur within a few hours or days. Immediate reactions include throat irritation, nasal congestion or cough, or more serious reactions. Delayed reactions may involve other parts of the body, and include nausea, dizziness, headache, flu-like symptoms, and eye irritations. Serious reaction can include nerve damage and choking.

One of the most common ways in which children are exposed to toxic substances is by drinking or swallowing them (ingestion), because they often put materials in their mouths. These materials may contain toxins, such as lead in paint or poison in plants. Providers are most likely to be exposed to toxins when they ingest contaminated liquids they have mistaken for water or juice.

Exposure through the skin is usually caused by improperly handling chemicals. Chemical exposure to skin can cause skin irritations, burns, and allergic reactions. Chemicals can also enter the bloodstream through cuts or sores. Some chemicals can penetrate the skin's natural protective coatings and enter the bloodstream. Once in the bloodstream, toxic chemicals can damage vital organs. To prevent toxic poisoning:

- Post emergency and poison control numbers in a visible place. (A list of regional poison control centers is included as Appendix 2.)
- Know first aid. (See the first aid chart in the Emergency Illness or Injury section.)
- Read chemical labels. Know the hazards.
- Choose the least hazardous product that can do the job.
- Choose multi-use products to cut down on the number of different chemicals you need to use and store.
- Use the smallest quantity required to do the job.
- Use the form of the chemical that most reduces risk of exposure, that is, use a cream instead of a liquid.
- Wear protective clothing, gloves, and safety glasses when using chemicals.
- Only use chemicals in well-ventilated areas.
- Never mix chemicals.
- Make sure labels remain attached to containers; don't pour chemicals into another container.
- Store chemicals in locked cabinets out of the reach of children.
- Know the hazards of common household products and how to safely handle them. (See chart below.)
- Keep household plants out of the reach of children.
- Use only lawn chemicals that the Environmental Protection Agency lists as "nonrestricted use."
- Use only arts and crafts materials that are nontoxic.

Hazards of Common Cleaning Products

Product	Can Cause	Hazard
Baking Soda	Eye irritation, redness, pain	Reacts with acids, such as vinegar.
Vinegar	Eye irritation, mild skin irritation	Reacts with bases (such as baking soda) and oxidizers (substances that easily give off oxygen such as chlorine); corrodes metals.
Ammonia (10%)	Severe eye irritation, swelling, burns, and possible blindness; corrosive skin burns and pain; nose and throat irritation, coughing, and chest pain if inhaled; burning pain to mouth, throat and stomach, vomiting, and shock if swallowed, and, if ammonia enters lungs, possible fatal fluid accumulation (only 1 oz. could be fatal if swallowed).	Never mix with bleach. Reacts violently with acids and other chemicals; corrodes metals.
Chlorine Bleach	Eye burns, blurred vision; skin redness, pain, drying, and cracking; sore throat, coughing, and labored breathing if inhaled; sore throat, vomiting, and burns if swallowed.	Reacts with acid or heat; produces chlorine gas; corrodes metals.

LEAD POISONING

Lead poisoning is a common environmental health problem among children. Even low blood lead levels can be harmful to children and have been associated with decreased intelligence as a longterm complication. Most children with elevated lead levels have no symptoms until they reach extreme levels. The only way to tell they have lead poisoning is to test their blood.

Young children, especially those 18-24 months old, are at greatest risk for lead poisoning because they often put their hands in their mouths and thus are more likely to eat dust, paint, and soil contaminated with lead. Children also absorb lead more easily. Because of their growth, development, and increased metabolism (the process the body uses to change nutrients to energy), children are more sensitive to the harmful health effects of lead.

Children can be exposed to lead by:

- Eating lead-based paint chips or dust or soil contaminated with lead-based paint or leaded gasoline. Most children get lead poisoning from breathing in lead-based paint dust or chewing on surfaces, such as windowsills or other surfaces close to the floor, that have been painted with lead-based paint. This usually happens in older homes, and especially those that are being or have recently been remodeled.

- Drinking water that has moved through lead pipes.
- Being exposed to lead dust carried by family workers who work with lead.
- Eating food served on lead-glazed pottery or improperly fired ceramic ware.
- Eating food taken from lead-soldered cans.
- Taking some traditional medicines that contain lead, such as greta or azarcon.
- Being exposed to lead through contamination of the environment by adult hobbies, such as making stained glass or pottery.

As a child care provider, you can help reduce children's risk of lead poisoning by:
- Washing children's hands frequently and before meals.
- Feeding children diets rich in iron and calcium, which will reduce the amount of lead absorbed from the gastrointestinal tract.
- Preparing and storing food in containers that do not release lead, such as those made of glass, stainless steel, or plastic. Never store food in opened cans. Only use ceramic containers that have labels saying they are made with lead-free glazes.
- Only using toys and arts and crafts materials that do not contain lead. Arts and crafts materials made after 1990 that are labeled "conforms to ASTM D-4236" and that have no health warnings are considered nontoxic.
- Relocating during remodeling projects that may create lead-based-paint dust.
- Having your facility evaluated for lead hazards if you believe it may be at risk. Older buildings with deteriorating paint carry a greater risk for lead hazards, as do buildings thought to have been a source of lead exposure for a child who has been diagnosed with lead poisoning. Lead paint concentrations were highest before 1950, but lead continued to be used in residential paint until 1978. To get further information on testing for lead and on preventing lead poisoning, call your state or local health department, the National Lead Information Hotline, (800) LEAD-FYI, or the National Lead Information Clearinghouse, (800) 424-LEAD.

AIR POLLUTION

Outdoor Air Pollution

Air quality has improved over the last 20 years, but air pollution is still an important health problem in many areas across the country, including most cities. The two most common pollutants are ozone (smog) and particulate matter (pollen, soot, dust, etc.). Children are very sensitive to the effects of air pollution. Children breathe more rapidly than do adults, and inhale more pollution per pound of body weight than adults. Therefore, their lungs have a greater chance for being exposed to harmful air pollutants. While exercising, children breathe more heavily and air pollution can be inhaled more deeply into the lungs. When children have a cold or are exercising, they often breathe through their mouths, taking in more pollutants than if the air was filtered through their noses. Because children's lungs are still developing, repeatedly breathing in polluted air may contribute to permanent lung damage.

You can help protect the children in your care from the harmful effects of air pollution by:

- Not conducting outdoor activities on days when the *air quality index* in your area is 100 or above. In communities where air pollution is a problem, this index is reported by local radio and television stations and newspapers.
- Scheduling outdoor activities for the early morning on smoggy days, especially in the summer. In many communities, summer smog levels peak in mid to late afternoon on hot days (over 90 degrees) when the air is stagnant.
- Conducting outdoor activities away from areas with heavy traffic.

Indoor Air Pollution

Because children spend a great deal of time indoors, the quality of air indoors is important, too. The greatest threat to indoor air is **tobacco smoke**. Without exception, cigarette smoking should not be allowed anywhere in a child care facility by anyone. Exposing children to second-hand smoke:

- harms children's lungs,
- increases the risk of ear infections,
- worsens the health of children with asthma, and
- exposes children to numerous cancer-causing chemicals.

Carbon monoxide is a particularly dangerous indoor air pollutant. You can't see it or smell it. High levels of carbon monoxide can cause headaches, dizziness, nausea, and weakness. At very high levels, carbon monoxide poisoning can cause death. But you can easily prevent these problems by maintaining furnaces and other appliances in good repair and by installing carbon monoxide detectors. Carbon monoxide detectors look like smoke detectors, are inexpensive, and are sold in hardware stores.

Wall-to-wall carpeting can contribute to poor indoor air because it can trap all sorts of chemicals, serve as a breeding ground for molds and microscopic organisms such as dust mites, and is difficult to clean. You do not need to remove carpeting if no problem exists. But if you plan to build a new child care facility or remodel an old one, you should consider installing smooth floors such as vinyl.

Radon is a colorless, odorless, radioactive gas formed by the breakdown of radium, a naturally occurring element in the earth. High radon levels have been found in every state. Radon can be found in soil, water, building materials, and natural gas. When a building settles, small cracks may form in the foundation. These cracks allow gases in the earth, including radon, to seep into a building. The greatest concentrations of radon are usually found in the basement or ground floor.

Radon breaks down into radioactive particles that can get trapped in your lungs when you breathe. As they break down further, these particles release small bursts of energy that can damage lung tissue. This can lead to lung cancer. Radon is the second leading cause of death from lung cancer in the United States. Only cigarette smoking causes more cases of death from lung cancer. Smokers are at a greater risk for lung cancer due to exposure to radon than are nonsmokers.

You need to determine if your facility or home has dangerous levels of radon by measuring the indoor air for radon. The amount of radon is measured in *picocuries per liter* of air. Testing for radon is very inexpensive. "Do it yourself" radon test kits are sold at hardware and other home improvement stores. Buy a kit that is certified by the Environmental Protection Agency or your state. You need to buy a radon test kit to measure the radon (in picocuries per liter of air) in your child care facility. Radon can be measured over different time periods ranging from 2 days to 1 year. Follow the manufacturer's instructions and mail the detector to the designated test laboratory. The laboratory will mail you the results. If the results are 4 picocuries per liter of air or higher, you need to take action to reduce the radon. For more information on how to reduce your radon health risk, contact your state radon office or call 1-800-SOS-RADON (English) or 1-800-SALUD-1-2 (Spanish).

Asbestos is a fire-resistant material that, in the past, was sprayed on ceilings, pipes, and other surfaces in buildings. Over time, asbestos becomes crumbly and flakes into a fine dust that hangs in the air. Asbestos is no longer used in new construction because it was found to cause serious lung problems and cancer. These problems can develop as late as 20 to 40 years after a person has been exposed to it. To prevent exposure to asbestos, the asbestos must be either sprayed with a sealant, enclosed with newly constructed walls or ceilings, or removed. Only qualified workers should remove asbestos. No one else should be present during the removal process. If you suspect your child care facility may have asbestos-lined building materials, contact your local health department to obtain information on how to have the air in your facility sampled and analyzed.

EXPOSURE TO ELECTRIC AND MAGNETIC FIELDS

Electric and magnetic fields (EMFs) are produced by voltage or electric pressure in power lines, electrical wiring, and electric devices. Both electric and magnetic fields exist near electric devices that are turned on. Objects that conduct electricity (e.g., trees, buildings, metal screen, and human skin) can reduce electric fields and thereby shield people under them. Shielding people from magnetic fields, however, is very difficult. Both magnetic and electric fields diminish with increasing distance from the source.

Studies to find out what effect exposure to electric and magnetic fields have on people's health have been inconclusive. Some study results have suggested that EMFs may have a bad effect on health (such as causing leukemia or other cancers) and some studies show no effect from exposure to EMFs. Most scientists do not believe that research results are convincing enough to warrant drastic action by homeowners, schools, or businesses.

If you are concerned about electric and magnetic fields in your child care facility (both indoors and outdoors), most power companies will measure the level of the fields free of charge and compare them to averages in other homes, schools, or businesses. You can reduce exposure to electric or magnetic fields generated by electric devices by keeping a distance from the devices when they are operating and by unplugging them when they are not in use. You can also reduce exposure by avoiding close proximity to sources of electric and magnetic fields that might be discovered by the power company when they make their measurements.

62

For further information, call or write the Superintendent of Documents, U.S. Government Printing Office, Washington, DC 20402, 202-512-1800 to obtain a copy of the pamphlet *Questions and Answers about EMF: Electric and Magnetic Fields Associated with the Use of Electric Power*, DOE/EE-0040, published by the National Institute of Environmental Health Sciences and the U.S. Department of Energy, January 1995.

EXPOSURE TO HEAT AND ULTRAVIOLET RAYS

Children are more likely than adults to be affected by heat and sunlight. They can more quickly lose body fluid and become dehydrated or develop heat stroke. Their sensitive skin also can be burned more easily by the sun's ultraviolet rays. Children can also be burned by objects or surfaces, particularly metal surfaces, that have been heated by the sun. Overexposure to the sun's harmful rays during childhood has been linked to skin and other cancers later in life. To reduce injuries caused by heat and sun:

- Limit the time that children spend outdoors during the hottest part of the day (10:00 a.m. to 2:00 p.m.)
- Require parents to provide sun block lotion with a sun protection factor (SPF) of at least 15 if children will be spending more than a few minutes in the sun.
- Provide drinks for children before, during, and after playing outdoors.
- Require that children wear protective clothing if they will be exposed to the sun for extended periods, such as on a field trip outdoors. Hats or sun visors, long-sleeved shirts and pants, and sun block lotion will prevent burns to sensitive skin.

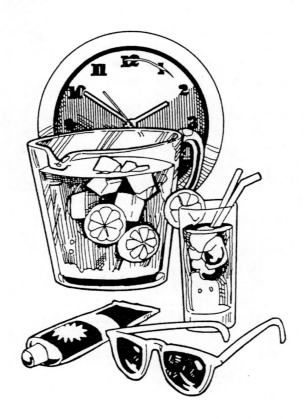

PETS

Many child care providers who care for children in their own homes have pets. Pets can be excellent companions for children. Pets can meet emotional needs of children and others for love and affection. Caring for pets also gives children an opportunity to learn how to treat and be responsible for others. However, some guidelines for protecting the health and safety of the children should be followed.

- All pets, whether kept indoors or outside, should be in good health, show no evidence of disease, and be friendly toward children.
- Dogs or cats should be appropriately immunized (check with the veterinarian) and be kept on flea, tick, and worm control programs. Proof of immunizations should be kept in a safe place.
- Pet living quarters should be kept clean. All pet waste should be disposed of immediately. Litter boxes should not be accessible to children.
- Child care providers should always be present when children play with pets.
- Children should be taught how to behave around a pet. They should be taught not to provoke the pet or remove the pet's food. They should always keep their faces away from a pet's mouth, beak, or claws.
- If you have a pet in your child care facility, tell parents before they enroll their child. Some children have allergies that may require the parents to find other child care arrangements.
- Children should wash their hands after handling pets or pet items.
- All reptiles carry Salmonella. Therefore, small reptiles that might be handled by children, including turtles and iguanas, can easily transmit Salmonella to them. Iguanas and turtles are not appropriate pets for child care centers.
- Some pets, particularly "exotic" pets such as some turtles, iguanas, venomous or aggressive snakes, spiders, and tropical fish, may not be appropriate in the child care setting. Check with a veterinarian if you are unsure whether a particular pet is appropriate for children. Check with the local health department for regulations and advice regarding pets in the child care setting.

the **A B C** s

of Safe and Healthy
Child Care

Fact Sheets

On Childhood

Diseases and Conditions

66

the **ABC**s
of Safe and Healthy
Child Care

What You Should Know About...
Asthma in the Child Care Setting

Asthma is a chronic breathing disorder and is the most common chronic health problem among children. Children with asthma have attacks of coughing, wheezing, and shortness of breath, which may be very serious. These symptoms are caused by spasms of the air passages in the lungs. The air passages swell, become inflamed, and fill with mucus, making breathing difficult. Many asthma attacks occur when children get respiratory infections, including infections caused by common cold viruses. Attacks can also be caused by:

- exposure to cigarette smoke,
- stress,
- strenuous exercise,
- weather conditions, including cold, windy, or rainy days,
- allergies to animals, dust, pollen, or mold,
- indoor air pollutants, such as paint, cleaning materials, chemicals, or perfumes, or
- outdoor air pollutants, such as ozone.

As with any child with a chronic condition, the child care provider and parents should discuss specific needs of the child and whether they can be sufficiently met by the provider. Some people believe that smaller-sized child care centers or family child care home environments may be more beneficial to a child with asthma because exposure to common respiratory viruses may be reduced. However, this has not been proven to be true.

Children with asthma may be prescribed medications to relax the small air passages and/or to prevent passages from becoming inflamed. These medications may need to be administered every day or only during attacks. Asthma medication is available in several forms, including liquid, powder, and pill, or it can be breathed in from an inhaler or compressor. The child care provider should be given clear instructions on how and when to administer all medications and the name and telephone number of the child's doctor.

The child care provider should be provided with and keep on file an asthma action plan for each child with asthma. An asthma action plan lists emergency information, activities or conditions likely to trigger an asthma attack, current medications being taken, medications to be administered by the child care provider, and steps to be followed if the child has an acute asthma attack. Additional support from the child's health care providers should be available to the child care provider as needed.

68

Most children with asthma can lead a normal life, but may often have to restrict their activity. Some preventive measures for reducing asthma attacks include:

- Avoiding allergic agents such as dust, plush carpets, feather pillows, and dog and cat dander. Installing low-pile carpets, vacuuming daily, and dusting frequently can help to reduce allergic agents. A child who is allergic to dogs or cats may need to be placed in a facility without pets.
- Stopping exercise if the child begins to breathe with difficulty or starts to wheeze.
- Avoiding strenuous exercise.
- Avoiding cold, damp weather. A child with asthma may need to be kept inside on cold, damp days or taken inside immediately if cold air triggers an attack.

If a child with asthma has trouble breathing:

1. Stop the child's activity and remove whatever is causing the allergic reaction, if you know what it is.
2. Calm the child; give medication prescribed, if any, for an attack.
3. Contact the parents.
4. If the child does not improve very quickly, and the parents are unavailable, call the child's doctor.
5. **If the child is unable to breathe, call 911.**
6. Record the asthma attack in the child's file. Describe the symptoms, how the child acted during the attack, what medicine was given, and what caused the attack, if known.

the **ABC**s
of Safe and Healthy
Child Care

What You Should Know About...
Baby Bottle Tooth Decay and Oral Health
in the Child Care Setting

Although the responsibility for a child's oral health rests with the parents, child care providers play an important role in maintaining the oral health of children in child care settings. Knowing a few basic oral health guidelines can greatly help a child care provider's ability to do so.

Although tooth decay is not as common as it used to be, it is still one of the most common diseases in children. Many children still get cavities. While fluoridated drinking water and fluoride-containing toothpaste have helped to improve the oral health of both children and adults, regular toothbrushing and a well-balanced diet are still very important to maintaining good oral health.

Primary, or baby, teeth commonly begin to come in or *erupt* in a baby's mouth at about 4 to 6 months of age and continue until all 20 have come in at about the age of 2-1/2 years. This eruption of primary teeth, or teething, can cause sore and tender gums that appear red and puffy. To relieve the soreness, give the baby a cold teething ring or washcloth to chew on. Teething medicine is not recommended.

Many primary teeth will not be replaced by permanent teeth for 10 to 12 years. Until that time, they need to be kept healthy to enable a child to chew food, speak, and have an attractive smile. Primary teeth are at risk for decay soon after they erupt. Tooth decay is caused by germs (bacteria) and sugars from food or liquids building up on a tooth. Over time, these bacteria dissolve the enamel, or outer layer, of the tooth. This damaged area is called a cavity. Regular brushing prevents the build-up of bacteria and sugars and the damage they cause.

Baby bottle tooth decay (or nursing bottle mouth) is a leading dental problem for children under 3 years of age. Baby bottle tooth decay occurs when a child's teeth are exposed to sugary liquids, such as formula, fruit juices, and other sweetened liquids for a continuous, extended period of time. The practice of putting a baby to bed with a bottle, which the baby can suck on for hours, is the major cause of this dental condition. The sugary liquid flows over the baby's upper front teeth and dissolves the enamel, causing decay that can lead to infection. The longer the practice continues, the greater the damage to the baby's teeth and mouth. Treatment is very expensive.

70

The American Academy of Pediatric Dentistry has developed the following guidelines for preventing baby bottle tooth decay:

- Don't allow a child to fall asleep with a bottle containing milk, formula, fruit juices, or other sweet liquids. Never let a child walk with a bottle in her mouth.
- Comfort a child who wants a bottle between regular feedings or during naps with a bottle filled with cool water.
- Always make sure a child's pacifier is clean and never dip a pacifier in a sweet liquid.
- Introduce children to a cup as they approach 1 year of age. Children should stop drinking from a bottle soon after their first birthday.
- Notify the parent of any unusual red or swollen areas in a child's mouth or any dark spot on a child's tooth so that the parent can consult the child's dentist.

To prevent infections from spreading through germs found in saliva and blood on toothbrushes, see "Using and Handling Toothbrushes" in the chapter, "Following Protective Practices to Reduce Disease and Injury."

the

of Safe and Healthy
Child Care

What You Should Know About...
Bacterial Meningitis in the Child Care Setting

Meningitis is an inflammation of the membranes that cover the brain and spinal cord. The cause of this inflammation is infection with either bacteria or viruses.

Meningitis caused by a bacterial infection (sometimes called spinal meningitis) is one of the most serious types, sometimes leading to permanent brain damage or even death. Bacterial meningitis is most commonly caused by bacteria called *Neisseria meningitidis* (meningococcal meningitis), *Streptococcus pneumoniae*, or *Haemophilus influenzae* serotype b (*H. flu* meningitis). These bacteria are carried in the upper back part of the throat (called the nasopharynx) of an infected person and are spread either through the air (when the person coughs or sneezes organisms into the air) or by direct contact with secretions from the nasopharynx of the infected person. However, transmission usually occurs only after very close contact with the infected person.

Symptoms of bacterial meningitis include sudden onset of fever, headache, neck pain or stiffness, vomiting (often without abdominal complaints), and irritability. These symptoms may quickly progress to decreased consciousness (difficulty in being aroused), convulsions, and death. For this reason, if any child displays symptoms of possible meningitis, he or she should receive medical care immediately.

Meningitis caused by *Haemophilus influenza* serotype b (Hib) can be prevented with Hib vaccine, which is part of routine childhood immunizations. Some cases of meningococcal meningitis can also be prevented by vaccine. However, this vaccine is not used routinely, and usually only during outbreaks or in high risk children.

Children with bacterial meningitis are almost always hospitalized. Providers are often told only that the child has meningitis and may not know the exact type.

If a child or adult in your child care facility is diagnosed with bacterial meningitis:

- Verify the type of meningitis involved. If a child in your care is diagnosed, contact the child's physician, explain that the child attends your facility, and you need to know the type of meningitis.
- If H.flu is involved, review immunization status of children to identify children who have not received their Hib vaccine.
- Immediately contact your local health department. Many states require that child care

facilities report suspected or known cases of bacterial meningitis. Your health department should also be able to recommend that you notify parents and potentially exposed persons as well as preventive antibiotics to reduce the risk of infections in exposed persons who may not be adequately vaccinated.

- Closely observe all remaining children and staff for any possible early signs of illness.
- IMMEDIATELY refer to a physician any exposed child or adult who develops fever, headache, rashes, spots, unusual behavior, or other symptoms of concern regardless of whether they have taken preventive antibiotics.
- Encourage close cooperation, support, and information sharing with staff and parents regarding measures being taken to reduce the risk of further transmission.

the **ABC**s

of Safe and Healthy
Child Care

What you should know about...
Campylobacter Infections in the Child Care Setting

Campylobacter infections are caused by a group of bacteria which are found in many different birds and mammals. While we once thought that this group only caused infections in other animals, we now know that the campylobacteria are responsible for a number of diseases, including diarrheal illness, in humans. Persons often become infected when they eat or drink foods or liquids contaminated with feces of infected animals. Similar exposure to human feces, especially from diapered children, may promote transmission in child care settings. Many people become infected from eating poorly cooked meats, especially poultry. Waterborne infections result from drinking water from contaminated wells, springs or streams, and this is a leading cause of diarrhea among backpackers in some parts of the United States.

Although outbreaks of campylobacter diarrhea have been reported from child care facilities, these are rare and child care providers are more likely to encounter this as a sporadic case. To prevent campylobacter infections in your facility:

- Make sure that all meats, especially poultry, are cooked completely before serving. Take care to avoid contaminating foods that will not be cooked with juice from raw meats and poultry.
- Practice good hygiene, especially careful handwashing after handling pets and cleaning their cages or pens.
- Isolate animals with diarrhea from children and take them to a veterinarian for diagnosis and treatment. However, these bacteria may also be present in feces of apparently healthy pets.
- Exclude children with diarrhea, especially those in diapers, from child care until their diarrhea resolves. Although campylobacter may be present in the feces for a few weeks after diarrhea has ceased, transmission is believed less likely than during diarrhea.
- Notify your state or local health department if you become aware that a child or adult in your facility has developed campylobacter. This infection is reportable in many states and there may be laws or regulations dealing with persons with campylobacter infections.

the ABCs
of Safe and Healthy
Child Care

What You Should Know About...
Chickenpox in the Child Care Setting

Chickenpox is a very contagious disease caused by the varicella zoster virus. Most children in the United States experience chickenpox before they are school-aged. A vaccine against chickenpox is now available. Although chickenpox is not a serious disease for most children, those whose immune systems are impaired (e.g., newborns and persons who are on chemotherapy for cancer, have AIDS, or take steroids like cortisone or prednisone) may experience severe disease, or even death. Chickenpox can also cause more severe health problems in pregnant women, causing stillbirths or birth defects, and can be spread to their babies during childbirth. Occasionally chickenpox can cause serious, life-threatening illnesses, such as encephalitis or pneumonia, especially in adults. In the past, some children who had chickenpox and were given aspirin developed Reye's Syndrome, which affects the liver and brain and results in the abrupt onset of seizures and, in some cases, death. For this and other reasons, aspirin should not be given to any child.

Chickenpox usually begins as an itchy rash of small red bumps on the scalp that spreads to the stomach or back before spreading to the face. However, this pattern can vary from person to person. It is believed to be spread person-to-person when a susceptible person is exposed to respiratory tract secretions (i.e., those produced by coughing or running noses) or directly to fluid from the open sores of an infected person. The disease is so contagious in its early stages that an exposed person who is not immune to the virus has a 70% to 80% chance of contracting the disease.

After infection, the virus stays in the body for life. Although people cannot get chickenpox twice, the same virus causes "shingles" or *herpes zoster*. An adult with shingles can spread the virus to someone, adult or child, who has not had chickenpox and the susceptible person can develop chickenpox. However, persons who have had chickenpox previously and are exposed outside child care are unlikely to bring the infection to child care unless they become ill.

If an adult or child develops chickenpox in the child care setting:

- Temporarily exclude the sick child or adult from the center. Allow the person to return 6 days after the rash begins or when all chickenpox blisters have formed scabs. (Local public health laws vary on the length of exclusion; consult your local health department.)
- Notify all staff members and parents that a case of chickenpox has occurred. Urge anyone who you know has an impaired immune system or who might be pregnant to consult a physician about the need for special preventive treatment.

- Contact the local health department to determine additional preventive measures. In some areas, child care providers are required to report known or suspected cases of chickenpox.

If a case of shingles occurs in the child care setting, the infected person should cover any lesions. If that is not possible, the person should be excluded from the child care setting until the lesions crust over.

the **ABC**s
of Safe and Healthy
Child Care

What You Should Know About...
Cold Sores in the Child Care Setting

Cold sores are usually caused by type 1 of the herpes simplex virus. Children often become infected with this virus in early childhood and many have no symptoms. When symptoms do occur, they may include fever, runny nose, and painful lesions (fever blisters or cold sores) on the lips or in the mouth. The blisters or cold sores usually form scabs and heal within a few days.

Cold sores are spread by direct contact with the lesions or saliva of an infected person. Spreading the virus within families is common.

To prevent the spread of herpes simplex virus in the child care setting:

- Make sure all children and adults in the facility use good handwashing practices.
- Do not allow children to share toys that can be put in their mouths. (Virus may be present even though sores are absent or not noticeable.)
- After a child has mouthed a toy, remove it from the play area and put it in a bin for toys to be disinfected at day's end.
- Only exclude a child with open blisters or mouth sores if the child is a biter, drools uncontrollably, or mouths toys that other children may in turn put in their mouths.
- Do not kiss the child or allow the child to kiss others where direct contact with the sore may occur.
- Use gloves if applying medicated ointment to the sore.

the **ABC**s
of Safe and Healthy
Child Care

What You Should Know About...
The Common Cold in the Child Care Setting

The common cold is caused by many different types of viruses. Usual symptoms can include sore throat, runny nose and watering eyes, sneezing, chills, and a general, all-over achiness.

Colds may be spread when a well person breathes in germs that an infected person has coughed, sneezed, or breathed into the air or when a well person comes in direct contact with the nose, mouth, or throat secretions of an infected person (for example, when a well person's hands touch a surface that the infected person has coughed or sneezed on).

To prevent the spread of colds:

- Make sure that all children and adults use good handwashing practices.
- Clean and disinfect all common surfaces and toys on a daily basis. (See "Cleaning and Disinfection" section.)
- Make sure the child care facility is well ventilated, either by opening windows or doors or by using a ventilation system to periodically exchange the air inside the child care facility.
- Make sure that children are not crowded together, especially during naps on floor mats or cots.
- Teach children to cover coughs and wipe noses using disposable tissues in a way that secretions are contained by the tissues and do not get on their hands.

Excluding children with mild respiratory infections, including colds, is generally not recommended as long as the child can participate comfortably and does not require a level of care that would jeopardize the health and safety of other children. Such exclusion is of little benefit since viruses are likely to be spread even before symptoms have appeared.

78

the **ABC**'s
of Safe and Healthy
Child Care

What You Should Know About...
Cryptosporidiosis in the Child Care Setting

Cryptosporidiosis is an infectious diarrheal disease caused by the Cryptosporidium parasite. Cryptosporidiosis is a common cause of diarrhea in children, especially those in child care settings. Symptoms usually include watery diarrhea and stomach ache, but can also include nausea and vomiting, general ill feeling, and fever. Healthy people who contract cryptosporidiosis almost always get better without any specific treatment. Symptoms can come and go for up to 30 days, but usually subside in less. However, cryptosporidiosis can cause severe illness in persons with compromised immune systems, such as those with HIV infection or those taking drugs that suppress the immune system.

Cryptosporidiosis is spread through fecal-oral transmission by feces of an infected person or an object that has been contaminated with the infected person's feces. Infection can also occur if someone ingests food or water contaminated with the parasite. Cryptosporidiosis outbreaks in child care settings are most common during late summer/early fall (August/September), but may occur at any time. The spread of cryptosporidiosis is highest among children who are not toilet-trained, and higher among toddlers than infants, probably due to the toddlers' increased movement and interaction among other children. For child care providers, the risk is greatest for those who change diapers.

Cryptosporidium is tougher to kill than most disease-causing organisms. The usual disinfectants, including most commonly used bleach solutions, have little effect on the Cryptosporidium parasite. An application of a 3-percent concentration of hydrogen peroxide or a 1-percent concentration of ammonia seem to be the best choices for disinfection during an outbreak of cryptosporidiosis. However, because ammonia has a strong odor and produces hazardous gas when mixed with bleach or other chlorinated solutions, hydrogen peroxide is probably the best choice in the child care setting.

If an outbreak of cryptosporidiosis occurs in the child-care setting:

- Contact your state or local health department. Health officials may require negative stool cultures from the infected child before allowing return to the child care setting.
- Exclude any child or adult with diarrhea until the diarrhea has ceased. Children who are infected with cryptosporidium but do not have diarrhea may be allowed to return.
- Make sure that everyone in the child care setting practices good handwashing technique, using disposable towels.

- Wash your hands after using the toilet, after helping a child use the toilet, and after diapering a child and before preparing or serving food. (Note: In larger facilities, when staffing permits, people who change diapers should not prepare or serve food.)
- Have children wash their hands upon arrival at your child care facility, after using the toilet, after having their diapers changed (an adult should wash an infant's or small child's hands), and before eating snacks or meals.
- Disinfect toys, bathrooms, and food preparation surfaces daily.
- Notify parents of children who have been in direct contact with a child who has diarrhea. Parents should contact the child's physician if their child develops diarrhea.
- Make sure children wear clothing over their diapers to reduce the opportunity for diarrheal leakage.
- Instead of a bleach solution, use a 3% concentration of hydrogen peroxide to soak possibly contaminated surfaces for 10 minutes to disinfect them. (This is not a routine measure, but may be necessary if an outbreak -- usually 2 or more cases in the same child care group-- occurs.)
- Notify any child care provider, the parents of any children, or any household contacts of a person known to have an impaired immune system. They should consult their physicians.

the ABCs
of Safe and Healthy
Child Care

What You Should Know About...
Cytomegalovirus (CMV) in the Child Care Setting

CMV is a virus with which most people eventually become infected. Children and staff in the child care setting are especially likely to be infected. Children usually have no symptoms when they become infected with CMV. Occasionally, older children in child care usually will develop an illness similar to mononucleosis, with a fever, sore throat, enlarged liver, and malaise. However, there is no reason to exclude a child excreting CMV from child care.

CMV is spread from person to person by direct contact with body fluids such as blood, urine, or saliva. Thus, it may be spread through intimate contact such as in diaper changing, kissing, feeding, bathing, and other activities where a healthy person comes in contact with the urine or saliva of an infected person. CMV can also be passed from the mother to the child before birth. Congenital infection with CMV can cause hearing loss, mental retardation, and other birth defects. Since the greatest risk of damage to a fetus occurs during a woman's first infection with CMV, women who have never been infected with CMV are at risk of delivering an infant with CMV disease if they become infected during pregnancy. Child care providers who are or may become pregnant should be carefully counseled about the potential risks to a developing fetus due to exposure to cytomegalovirus.

Female child care providers who expect to become pregnant should:

- Be tested for antibodies to CMV.
- If test shows no evidence of previous CMV infection, reduce contact with infected children by working, at least temporarily, with children age 2 years or older, among whom there is far less virus circulation.
- Carefully wash their hands with warm water and soap after each diaper change and contact with children's saliva.
- Avoid contact with children's saliva by not kissing children on the lips and by not placing children's hands, fingers, toys, and other saliva-laden objects in their own mouths.

Note: Contact with children that does not involve exposure to saliva or urine poses no risk to a mother or child care provider and should not be avoided out of fear of potential infection with CMV.

the **ABC**s
of Safe and Healthy
Child Care

What You Should Know About...
Diarrheal Diseases in the Child Care Setting

Diarrhea can be caused by a variety of different germs, including bacteria, viruses, and parasites. However, children can sometimes have diarrhea without having an infection, such as when diarrhea is caused by food allergies or as a result of taking medicines such as antibiotics. A child should be considered to have diarrhea when the child's bowel movements are both more frequent than usual and looser and more watery than usual.

Children with diarrhea may have additional symptoms including nausea, vomiting, stomach aches, headache, or fever. **Children who are not toilet trained and have diarrhea should be excluded from child care settings regardless of the cause.**

Diarrhea is spread from person to person when a person touches the stool of an infected person or an object contaminated with the stool of an infected person and then ingests the germs, usually by touching the mouth with a contaminated hand. Diarrhea can also be spread by contaminated food. For more information on how to prevent foodborne diseases, see the information sheet, " Foodborne Diseases in the Child Care Setting" in this section. Children in diapers and child care providers who change their diapers have an increased risk of diarrheal diseases.

To prevent diarrheal diseases from spreading in the child care setting:

- Exclude any child or adult who has diarrhea until these symptoms are gone.
- Make sure that everyone in the child care setting practices good handwashing technique.
- Wash your hands after using the toilet, helping a child use the toilet, and diapering a child and before preparing, serving, or eating food.
- Have children wash their hands upon arrival at your child care facility, after using the toilet, after having their diapers changed (an adult should wash an infant's or small child's hands), and before eating snacks or meals.
- Disinfect toys, bathrooms, and food preparation surfaces daily.
- Use disposable paper towels for handwashing.
- Notify parents of children who have been in direct contact with a child who has diarrhea. Parents should contact the child's physician if their child develops diarrhea.
- Use disposable table liners on changing tables and disinfect tables after each use.
- If at all possible, the person who prepares and/or serves food should not change diapers.
- If possible, diapered children should be cared for by different caregivers in a room

separate from toilet-trained children.
- Use diapers with waterproof outer covers that can contain liquid stool or urine, or use plastic pants
- Make sure that children always wear clothes over diapers.

Notify the local health department if two or more children in one classroom or home have diarrhea within a 48-hour period. Also notify the local health department if you learn that a child in your care has diarrhea due to *Shigella, Campylobacter, Salmonella, Giardia, Cryptosporidium,* or *Escherichia (E). coli.* Any child with prolonged or severe diarrhea or diarrhea with fever, or a known exposure to someone with infectious diarrhea, should be seen by a health care provider.

the ABCs
of Safe and Healthy
Child Care

What You Should Know About...
Diphtheria in the Child Care Setting

Diphtheria is a disease caused by a bacteria, *Corynebacterium diphtheriae,* which invades the throat. Diphtheria is usually spread through the airborne route or through contact with saliva or nasal secretions of an infected person. Up-to-date vaccination with the DTP (diphtheria is the "D") vaccine can prevent this very serious, life-threatening disease.

Because almost all children are vaccinated, diphtheria is now rare in the United States. However, some children are not adequately vaccinated and cases still can occur. To prevent its spread in a child care setting:

- Review immunization records of all children upon admission and periodically thereafter. Any child whose immunizations are incomplete or not up-to-date should be referred to the health department or the child's physician for proper immunization.

- Upon notification by a parent or health care worker that a child absent from the child care setting has contracted diphtheria, immediately contact the local health department for instructions on preventive measures to be taken. The local health department may advise caregivers to closely observe all children and adults in the child care setting for sore throats for 7 days (the incubation period), request that anyone developing a sore throat see a physician, prescribe antibiotics for close contacts, and carefully observe group separation and good hygiene procedures.

the **ABC**s
of Safe and Healthy
Child Care

What You Should Know About...
Earache (Otitis Media) in the Child Care Setting

An earache or ear infection (otitis media) is usually a complication of an upper respiratory infection, such as a cold. Otitis media usually occurs in children under 3 years of age. Symptoms include inflammation of the middle ear, often with fluid building up behind the ear drum. The child may cry persistently, tug at the ear, have a fever, be irritable, and be unable to hear well. These symptoms may sometimes be accompanied by diarrhea, nausea, and vomiting. Otitis media is common in young children whether they attend child care or are cared for at home. However, some children appear to be more susceptible to otitis media than other children.

Otitis media is not contagious, but the upper respiratory illnesses that can lead to otitis media are infectious. Upper respiratory infections are spread when one person comes in contact with the respiratory secretions of an infected person which have contaminated the air or an object.

Otitis media is often treated with antibiotics. Some doctors give children daily antibiotics to prevent otitis media in children who have had repeat cases. Some children with chronic infections may require an operation to insert a tube to drain the fluid from the ear.

A child with an earache does not need to be excluded from the child care setting unless the child is too ill to participate in normal activities or needs more care than the provider can give without compromising the care given to the other children.

To help prevent the upper respiratory infections, which may lead to otitis media:

- Teach children to cover their mouths with a disposable tissue when they cough and blow their noses with disposable tissues.
- Only use a tissue once and then immediately throw it away.
- Do not allow children to share toys that they put in their mouths.
- After a child has discarded a toy that can be put in the mouth, pick it up and put it in a bin for dirty toys that is out of reach of the children. Wash and disinfect these toys before allowing children to play with them again. (See section on "Cleaning and Disinfection" in the chapter on "Protective Practices.")
- Make sure all children and adults use good handwashing practices. (See section on "Handwashing" in the chapter on "Protective Practices.")

the **ABC**s
of Safe and Healthy
Child Care

What you should know about...

E. coli O157:H7 **infections in the Child Care Setting**

Escherichia (E.) coli bacteria are found in the digestive tracts of most humans and many animals. Usually, these infections are harmless and may even be beneficial. Not all *E. coli* are alike and, in a few cases, illness may result from infection with particular strains. One strain, *E. coli* O157:H7, causes one of the most serious digestive tract infections in the United States. Some persons infected with this strain may have very mild illness while others develop severe bloody diarrhea. In some instances, infection may result in widespread breakdown of red blood cells leading to an often fatal, hemolytic uremic syndrome (HUS).

Infections with this organism are often the result of eating undercooked meat (especially hamburger). However, feces may also spread this infection and children and staff may pick it up from ill persons in child care facilities. To prevent the spread of *E. coli* O157:H7 infections in your child care facility:

- Practice good hygiene and careful handwashing.
- Make sure that meats, especially hamburger, served in child care facilities are cooked well done.
- Exclude from child care children, especially those in diapers, with diarrhea or loose stools until their diarrhea has resolved. Request that parents take any child with bloody diarrhea to a physician for evaluation.
- Notify your state or local health department of any child with bloody diarrhea. The health department may require that a person infected with *E. coli* O157:H7 demonstrate that they are no longer infectious before allowing them to return to work or child care.

the **ABC**s
of Safe and Healthy
Child Care

What You Should Know About...
Fifth Disease in the Child Care Setting

Fifth disease, also called erythema infectiosum or "slapped cheek disease," is an infection caused by parvovirus B19. Outbreaks most often occur in winter and spring, but a person may become ill with fifth disease at any time of the year. Symptoms begin with a mild fever and complaints of tiredness. After a few days, the cheeks take on a flushed appearance that looks like the face has been slapped. There may also be a lacy rash on the trunk, arms, and legs. Not all infected persons develop a rash.

Most persons who get fifth disease are not very ill and recover without any serious consequences. However, children with sickle cell anemia, chronic anemia, or an impaired immune system may become seriously ill when infected with parvovirus B19 and require medical care.

If a pregnant woman becomes infected with parvovirus B19, the fetus may suffer damage, including the possibility of stillbirth. The woman herself may have no symptoms or a mild illness with rash or joint pains.

Fifth disease is believed to be spread through direct contact or by breathing in respiratory secretions from an infected person. The period of infectiousness is before the onset of the rash. Once the rash appears, a person is no longer contagious. Therefore, a child who has been diagnosed with fifth disease need not be excluded from child care.

If an outbreak of fifth disease occurs in the child care setting:

- Notify all parents. Pregnant women and parents of children who have an impaired immune system, sickle cell anemia, or other blood disorders may want to consult their physicians.
- Make sure that all children and adults use good handwashing techniques. (See section on "Handwashing" in chapter on "Protective Practices.")

the **ABC**s
of Safe and Healthy
Child Care

What You Should Know About...
Foodborne Illnesses in the Child Care Setting

Food safety and sanitation are important aspects of providing healthy food for children. Improper food preparation, handling, or storage can quickly result in food being contaminated with germs that may lead to illness such as hepatitis A or diarrheal diseases if the contaminated food is eaten. Contact your local health department to obtain the local regulations and standards for food safety and sanitation and to ask about the availability of a food handler course in your area.

Understanding and following a few basic principles can help prevent food spoilage and transmission of infections. *To prevent foodborne infections:*

- Keep food at safe serving and storage temperatures at all times to prevent spoiling and the risk of transmitting disease. Food should be kept at 40°F or colder or at 140°F or warmer. The range between 40°F and 140°F is considered the "danger zone" because within this range bacteria grow most easily. Leftovers, including hot foods such as soups or sauces, should be refrigerated immediately and should not be left to cool at room temperature. Using shallow pans or bowls will facilitate rapid cooling. Frozen foods should be thawed in the refrigerator, not on counter tops, or in the sink with COLD water, not hot or warm water.
- Use only approved food preparation equipment, dishes, and utensils. Check local child care licensing regulations. Only use cutting boards that can be disinfected (made of nonporous materials such as glass, formica, or plastic), and use separate boards for ready-to-eat foods (including foods to be eaten raw) and for foods which are to be cooked, such as meats.
- Use proper handwashing techniques. Proper handwashing is important for everyone in a child-care setting, but is especially necessary for food handlers to prevent the spread of infections or contamination of the food.
- Don't handle food if you change diapers. In a large child care setting, food handlers should not change diapers and should avoid other types of contact that may contaminate their hands with infectious secretions. This may not be practical in a small child care setting in which the provider must also prepare the food. In this case, proper handwashing is essential.
- Don't prepare or serve food if you have diarrhea, unusually loose stools, or any other gastrointestinal symptoms of an illness, or if you have infected skin sores or injuries, or

open cuts. Small, uninfected cuts may be covered with nonporous, latex gloves.

- Supervise meal and snack times to make sure children do not share plates, utensils, or food that is not individually wrapped.
- Eating utensils that are dropped on the floor should be washed with soap and water before using .
- Discard food that is dropped on the floor and remove leftovers from the eating area after each snack or meal.
- Clean, sanitize, and properly store food service equipment and supplies. Follow dishwashing techniques as specified in the "Protective Practices" section of this handbook. Use only utensils and dishes that have been washed in a dishwasher or, if washed by hand, with sanitizers and disinfectants approved for this use. Otherwise, use disposable, single-use articles that are discarded after each use.
- Clean and sanitize after each use table tops on which food is served.
- Only accept expressed breast milk that is fresh and properly labeled with the child's name. Expressed breast milk to be used during the current shift should accompany the child that day. Don't store breast milk at the facility overnight. Send any unused expressed breast milk home with the child that day. NEVER feed a child breast milk unless it is labeled with that child's name.
- Except for an individual child's lunch, only accept food that is commercially prepared to be brought into the child care setting. Numerous institutional outbreaks of gastrointestinal illness, including infectious hepatitis, have been linked to consumption of home-prepared foods. Food brought into the child care setting to celebrate birthdays, holidays, or other special occasions should be obtained from commercial sources approved and inspected by the local health authority.
- Each individual child's lunch brought from home should be clearly labeled with the child's name, the date, and the type of food it is. It should be stored at an appropriate temperature until it is eaten. Food brought from a child's home should not be fed to another child.
- Raw eggs can be contaminated with Salmonella. No foods containing raw eggs should be served, including homemade ice cream made with raw eggs.

the **ABC**s
of Safe and Healthy
Child Care

What You Should Know About...
Giardiasis in the Child Care Setting

Giardiasis is a diarrheal illness caused by a parasite, *Giardia lamblia*. Many children infected with *giardia* have no symptoms. Other children may have foul-smelling, greasy diarrhea, gas, stomach aches, fatigue, and weight loss. *Giardia* can easily be spread in the child's home and parents and siblings may become infected.

Giardia is spread from person to person when a person touches the stool of or an object which has been contaminated by the stool of an infected person and then ingests the germs. Infection is often spread by not properly washing hands after bowel movements, after changing diapers, or before preparing foods. Giardia may also be transmitted through contaminated water, such as in water play tables. Outbreaks have also been linked to portable wading pools and contaminated water supplies.

To prevent the spread of giardiasis in your child care facility:

- Exclude any child or adult with acute diarrhea.
- Make sure that all children and adults practice good handwashing technique, using paper towels.
- In a large child care facility, the person preparing food should not change diapers.
- In a small child care facility, the child care provider should carefully wash hands after changing diapers and before handling foods.
- If possible, keep diapered children apart from toilet-trained children.
- Wash and disinfect toys that can be put in a child's mouth after each child's use. Refer to the discussion on cleaning toys in the "Disinfection" section of the chapter on "Protective Practices."
- Use diapers that can contain liquid stool or urine.
- Make sure that diapers have waterproof outer covers or use plastic pants.
- Children should wear clothes over diapers.
- Do not use portable wading pools.
- Wash children's hands before they use water play tables.

the ABCs
of Safe and Healthy
Child Care

What You Should Know About...
Hand-Foot-and-Mouth Disease (Coxsackie A) in the Child Care Setting

Hand-foot-and-mouth disease is a common childhood illness caused by coxsackievirus A16. In many people, infection with the virus causes mild or no symptoms. In others, infection may result in painful blisters in the mouth, on the gums and tongue, on the palms and fingers of the hand, or on the soles of the feet. The fluid in these blisters contains the virus, and symptoms may last for 7 to 10 days. The infection usually goes away without any serious complications.

Hand-foot-and-mouth disease can be spread when the virus present in the blisters is passed to another person. The virus can be passed through saliva from blisters in the mouth, through the fluid from blisters on the hands and feet, or through the infected person's feces.

Outbreaks in child care facilities usually coincide with an increased number of cases in the community. If an outbreak occurs in the child care setting:

- Make sure that all children and adults use good handwashing technique. (See "handwashing" in chapter on "Protective Practices.")
- Do not exclude ill persons because exclusion may not prevent additional cases since the virus may be excreted for weeks after the symptoms have disappeared. Also, some persons excreting the virus may have no symptoms. However, some benefit may be gained by excluding children who have blisters in their mouths and drool or who have weeping lesions on their hands.

the **ABC**s
of Safe and Healthy
Child Care

What You Should Know About...
Head Lice in the Child Care Setting

Head lice are tiny insects that live primarily on the head and scalp. They should not be confused with body lice, which may be found in clothing and bedding as well as on the body, or crab lice that infest the pubic area. They are found only on humans and should not be confused with fleas, which may be found on dogs, cats, and other pets.

Although small, adult head lice may be seen with the naked eye. Because lice move rapidly and only a few may be present, using a hand lens or magnifying glass may allow them to be seen more easily. Head lice suck blood, and the rash caused by their feeding activities may be more noticeable than the insects themselves. Head lice attach their eggs at the base of a hair shaft. These eggs, or nits, appear as tiny white or dark ovals and are especially noticeable on the back of the neck and around the ears. Adult head lice cannot survive for more than 48 hours apart from the human host.

Head lice are primarily spread through direct head to head contact, although sharing personal items such as hats, brushes, combs, and linens may play a role in their spread between children. Children with head lice should be treated with a medicated shampoo, rinse, or lotion developed specifically for head lice. *These treatments are very powerful insecticides and may be toxic if not used only as recommended.* The need to remove nits or egg capsules is controversial. Those found more than 1/4 inch from the scalp probably have already hatched or are not going to hatch. Treatments containing permethrin (an insecticide) have a high residual activity and are usually effective in killing nits as well as adult lice.

To prevent the spread of head lice when a case occurs in the child care setting:

- Temporarily exclude the infested child from the child care setting until 24 hours after treatment. Many state and local health departments require that children be free of nits before readmission. To assure effective treatment, check previously treated children for any evidence of new infection daily for 10 days after treatment. Repeat treatment in 7 to 10 days may be necessary.
- Nits can be removed using a fine-toothed comb. (A pet flea comb may work best.) Some commercial products may make removing nits easier. Commercial preparations to remove nits should be used according to the manufacturer's recommendations to assure that the residual activity of the insecticide is not affected.

92

- On the same day, screen all children in the classroom or group and any siblings in other classrooms for adult lice or nits. Children found to be infested should also be excluded and treated. Simultaneous treatment of all infested children is necessary to prevent spread back to previously treated children.
- Educate parents regarding the importance of following through with the same recommendations at home and notifying the facility if head lice have been found on any member of the household.
- Although head lice are not able to survive off of humans for more than a few days, many persons recommend washing clothes (including hats and scarves) and bedding in very hot water, and vacuuming carpets and upholstered furniture in rooms used by person infested with these insects. Combs and hair brushes may be soaked in hot (65°C) water for at least one hour. Flea bombs and other environmental insecticides are not effective against head lice.

the **ABC**s
of Safe and Healthy
Child Care

What You Should Know About...
Hepatitis A in the Child Care Setting

Hepatitis A is an infection of the liver caused by the hepatitis A virus (HAV). Young children often have no symptoms or very mild symptoms of disease. Adults and older children are more likely to have typical symptoms, which include fever, loss of appetite, nausea, diarrhea, and generally ill feeling (malaise). The skin and whites of the eyes take on a yellow color (jaundice). A person who has no symptoms is still infectious to others.

HAV is spread by the fecal-oral route. This means the disease is spread by putting something in the mouth that has been contaminated with the stool of an infected person. It can also be spread when a person eats food or drinks beverages which have been handled by a person infected with HAV and not subsequently cooked. Outbreaks of hepatitis A among children attending child care centers and persons employed at these centers have been recognized since the 1970s. Because infection among children is usually mild or asymptomatic and people are infectious before they develop symptoms, outbreaks are often only recognized when adult contacts (usually parents) become ill. Poor hygienic practices among staff who change diapers and also prepare food contribute to the spread of hepatitis A. Children in diapers are likely to spread the diseases because of contact with contaminated feces. Outbreaks rarely occur in child care settings serving only toilet-trained children.

A new vaccine is available to prevent hepatitis A , but is not currently licensed for children less than 2 years of age. Although hepatitis A outbreaks sometimes occur in child care settings, they do not happen often enough to make it necessary for child care providers or children attending child care to be routinely vaccinated against hepatitis A. When outbreaks occur in child care settings, gamma globulin may be administered to children, providers, and families of child care attendees to to limit transmission of hepatitis A.

If a child or adult in your child care facility is diagnosed with hepatitis A:

- Exclude the child or adult from the child care setting until 1 week after onset of symptoms.
- Immediately notify your local health department and request advice. Gamma globulin, if administered within the first 2 weeks after exposure, can prevent the infection from spreading to other children and families.
- Use good handwashing and hygiene practices.

the **ABC**s
of Safe and Healthy
Child Care

What You Should Know About...
Hepatitis B in the Child Care Setting

Hepatitis B is an infection of the liver caused by the hepatitis B virus (HBV). This virus is completely different from hepatitis A. Only about 10 percent of children who become infected with HBV show any symptoms. When children do have symptoms, they may be similar to those for hepatitis A: fatigue, loss of appetite, jaundice, dark urine, light stools, nausea, vomiting, and abdominal pain. However, hepatitis B is a much more serious infection. After infection with HBV, chronic infection develops in 70% to 90% of infants, 15% to 25% of 1- to 4-year-old children, and 5% to 10% of older children and adults. Premature death from cirrhosis or liver cancer occurs in 15% to 25% of persons with chronic infection. Persons who develop chronic HBV infection may remain infectious for the rest of their lives.

HBV infection is most commonly spread:

- By infected mothers to newborn infants through blood exposure at birth.
- By sharing contaminated needles during intravenous drug abuse.
- Through sexual intercourse.
- Through exposure of cuts or mucous membranes to contaminated blood.

HBV infection can also be transmitted if infected blood or body fluids come in contact with nonintact skin of an uninfected person, such as by biting, if the skin is broken. However, this is rare.

Hepatitis B is vaccine-preventable. **All infants should be vaccinated with three doses of hepatitis B vaccine during the first 18 months of life.** A child not previously vaccinated should receive three doses of vaccine by the age of 11 or 12 years. Child care providers should discuss with their doctor whether it is appropriate for them to receive hepatitis B vaccine.

To reduce the spread of hepatitis B:

- Require parents to submit up-to-date immunization certificates when previous certificates expire.
- Make sure that all children and adults use good handwashing practices.
- Do not allow children to share toothbrushes.
- Clean up blood spills immediately.

- Wear gloves when cleaning up blood spills unless the spill is so small it can be contained in the cloth or towel being used to clean it up.
- Wear gloves when changing a diaper soiled with bloody stools.
- Disinfect any surfaces on which blood has been spilled, using freshly prepared bleach solution.
- If a child care provider has open sores, cuts, or other abrasions on the hands, the provider should wear gloves when changing diapers or cleaning up blood spills.
- Observe children for aggressive behavior, such as biting. A child who is a chronic HBV carrier should be evaluated by a team that includes the child's parents or guardians, the child's physician, public health personnel, the proposed child care provider, and others to determine the most appropriate child care setting. This evaluation should consider the behavior, neurologic development, and physical condition of the child and the expected type of interaction with others in the child care setting. In each case, risks and benefits to both the infected child and to others in the child care setting should be weighed.

the **ABC**s
of Safe and Healthy
Child Care

What You Should Know About...
Human Immunodeficiency Virus Infections
in the Child Care Setting

When a person is first infected with the human immunodeficiency virus (HIV), he or she may have no symptoms or may become ill with a fever, night sweats, sore throat, general tiredness, swollen lymph glands, and a skin rash lasting for a few days to a few weeks. These early symptoms then go away by themselves. However, the virus stays in the body (becomes a chronic infection) and causes increasing loss of immune function that results in the body becoming unable to fight off infections to which we are all normally exposed. The late stage of this infection is called acquired immunodeficiency syndrome (AIDS). A person who is infected becomes potentially infectious to others for life.

Early symptoms of HIV infection in children include failure to grow and gain weight, chronic diarrhea without a specific cause, enlarged liver and spleen, swollen lymph glands, chronic thrush (yeast infections) and *Candida* (yeast) skin infections, pneumonia, and other bacterial, viral, fungal, and parasitic infections that healthy children do not usually get. However, many children are infected with HIV for many years before developing any symptoms.

HIV is not easily transmitted. HIV is most commonly spread:

- By sharing contaminated needles for intravenous drug abuse.
- Through sexual intercourse.
- By infected pregnant women to the fetus.
- By exposure to infected blood through a blood transfusion.

Less commonly, HIV may be spread:

- By infected mothers who breastfeed their infants.
- Occupationally to health care workers, primarily after being stuck with a needle containing HIV in infected blood.
- By exposure of open skin or mucous membranes to HIV contaminated body fluids. (Although it is very rare, a few cases have been reported in which HIV was spread by contact with blood or other body fluids from an infected person.)

No vaccine against HIV is available. However, HIV is not likely to be spread from one child to another in a child care setting, and no such case has ever been reported. The family home provider or center director should be informed by the child's parents or guardians when an HIV-positive child is admitted to child care. Because of concern over stigmatization, the person aware of a child's HIV infection should be limited to those who need such knowledge to care for the children in the child care setting. In situations where there is concern about the possibility of exposure of others to infected blood or other body fluids, a child who is infected with HIV should be evaluated by a team that includes the child's parents or guardians, the child's physician, public health personnel, and the proposed child care provider to determine the most appropriate child care setting. This evaluation should consider the behavior, neurologic development, and physical condition of the child and the expected type of interaction with others in the child care setting. In each case, risks and benefits to both the infected child and to others in the child care setting should be weighed.

Children with HIV infection need to be closely monitored by their physicians because they are more susceptible to severe manifestations of infectious illnesses than are other children. Children with HIV infection should receive childhood vaccinations (diphtheria-pertussis-tetanus vaccine, measles-mumps-rubella vaccine, inactivated polio vaccine, *Haemophilus* b conjugate vaccine, influenza vaccine, and pneumococcal vaccine) following the immunization schedule. Parents of children with weakened immune systems, whether due to HIV infection or other causes, should be advised when certain infectious diseases, such as cryptosporidiosis and fifth disease, have occurred in the child care setting. Such children may need to be removed from the child care setting until the outbreak has subsided in order to protect them from infections that could have severe complications for them.

If a child care provider has a weakened immune system, he or she should discuss with his or her physician precautions to be taken to avoid becoming infected with the many infections that young children are likely to transmit.

To reduce the risk of spread of HIV in the child care setting, all child care providers should routinely follow precautions necessary to prevent the spread of any bloodborne infection (including hepatitis B):

- Make sure all children and adults use good handwashing practices.
- Make sure all adults use good diapering practices.
- Wear gloves when changing a diaper soiled with bloody stools.
- Wash skin on which breastmilk has spilled with soap and water immediately.
- Do not allow children to share toothbrushes.
- Clean up blood spills immediately.
- Wear gloves when cleaning up blood and body fluid spills unless the spill is so small it can be contained in the cloth or towel being used to clean it up.
- Disinfect any surfaces on which blood or body fluids have been spilled with freshly prepared bleach solution.
- If a child care provider has open sores, cuts, or other abrasions on the hands, wear gloves when changing diapers or cleaning up blood spills.
- Cover open wounds on children and adults.

You should develop policies and procedures to follow in the event of an exposure to HIV. See procedures for HIV exposure through expressed breast milk or other body fluids in Nutrition and Foods Brought from Home section. A person who has had a severe exposure may need to be treated with antiviral drugs.

the A B C s
of Safe and Healthy
Child Care

What You Should Know About...
Impetigo in the Child Care Setting

Impetigo is a skin infection usually caused by one of two types of bacteria, group A streptococci and *Staphylococcus aureus*. Impetigo appears as a blistery rash. When the blisters open, they produce a thick, golden-yellow discharge that dries, crusts, and adheres to the skin.

Impetigo is spread from person to person through direct contact with the discharge from the lesions. This infection can rapidly spread among persons in close contact, such as children in a child care facility.

If a child in your facility has impetigo:

- Exclude the child from the center until 24 hours after treatment has begun and the child no longer has a discharge.
- Infected areas should be washed with mild soap and running water.
- Wash the infected child's clothes, linens, and towels at least once a day and never share them with other children.
- Wear gloves while applying any antibiotic ointment that a physician may recommend, and wash your hands afterwards. (Antibiotics taken by mouth may also be prescribed.)
- Make sure policies on cleaning and disinfecting toys are followed.

the ABCs
of Safe and Healthy
Child Care

What You Should Know About...
Infectious Mononucleosis in the Child Care Setting

Infectious mononucleosis is caused by the Epstein-Barr virus (EBV). EBV is believed to be present in saliva. Most young children infected with EBV show no symptoms, unlike older children and adults, who may have fever, fatigue, enlarged neck lymph nodes, and inflamed throat and tonsils.

Infectious mononucleosis is spread from person to person through contact with the saliva of an infected person. The virus spreads more rapidly among children in closed or overcrowded conditions. Most adults have been exposed to EBV by the age of 18 years and are immune.

If a person in your facility develops infectious mononucleosis:

- The infected person may return to the child care setting when he or she is able to participate in usual activities.
- Make sure all children and adults do not share eating or drinking utensils.
- Make sure all children and adults follow good handwashing practices.

100

the ABC s
of Safe and Healthy
Child Care

What You Should Know About...
Influenza in the Child Care Setting

Influenza (sometimes called "the flu") is a potentially serious viral disease that can make people of any age ill. Influenza can cause fever, chills, cough, sore throat, headache, and muscle aches. The influenza virus is usually passed when an infected person coughs or sneezes and another person inhales droplets containing the virus. Although most people are ill for only a few days, some have much more serious illness and need to be hospitalized. Thousands of people die each year from influenza-related complications. Most influenza-related deaths are in the elderly.

Anyone who wants to reduce their chance of catching influenza may receive the vaccination. Since the influenza virus changes frequently, yearly vaccination in October to early November is recommended for protection from influenza. Influenza vaccination is recommended for all adults in the child care setting, especially those who are in any of the following high risk categories:

- 65 years of age and over.
- Have chronic lung or heart disease.
- Require regular medical care for chronic metabolic (including diabetes mellitus), kidney, blood, or suppressed immune system diseases.
- Live or work with people who are in any of the above categories (or with children on long-term aspirin therapy.)

Any child 6 months and older can be vaccinated against influenza. Children in the following groups are at high risk of serious disease with influenza and should be vaccinated:

- Have chronic lung (including asthma) or heart disease.
- Require regular medical care for chronic metabolic (including diabetes mellitus), kidney, blood, or suppressed immune system diseases.
- Are on long-term aspirin therapy.
- Children who are in frequent contact, at home or in the child care setting, with people who are in any of the above high-risk categories should be vaccinated against influenza.

If a child or staff person develops a fever (100°F or higher under the arm, 101° orally, or 102° rectally) AND chills, cough, sore throat, headache, or muscle aches, he or she should be sent home.

During an epidemic of influenza you should:

- Closely observe all children for symptoms and refer anyone developing symptoms to his or her physician.
- Make sure all children and adults follow good handwashing and hygiene practices, including use and proper disposal of paper tissues.
- Make sure all children and adults follow good handwashing and hygiene practices, including use and proper disposal of paper tissues.
- In large facilities, follow appropriate group separation practices.
- Closely observe all children for symptoms and refer anyone developing symptoms to his or her physician.
- Notify parents.

the **ABC**s
of Safe and Healthy
Child Care

What You Should Know About...
Measles in the Child Care Setting

Measles is caused by the measles virus. Symptoms include a fever, runny nose, cough, and sore and reddened eyes followed by a red-brown blotchy rash. The rash usually starts on the face and spreads down the body, and lasts 3 or more days. Most children with measles become quite ill, but recover with no ill effects. Occasionally, however, measles can lead to pneumonia or inflammation of the brain and permanent disability or death. Adults and very young children tend to have more severe illness.

Measles is vaccine preventable. Measles vaccine is administered as part of the MMR (measles, mumps, rubella) vaccine series to children beginning at 12 to 15 months and again at 4 to 6 years of age or 11 to 12 years of age.

Measles is highly contagious and is spread easily from person to person through the air when an infected person coughs or sneezes and a susceptible person inhales the organism. These particles may remain suspended in the air, and persons have become infected simply be being in a room after an infected person has left. Thus, all children and any adult who did not have the disease as a child should be vaccinated. Adults born prior to 1957 are considered immune. Child care providers born after 1956 should receive 2 doses of MMR vaccine, with at least one dose given after 1967 at age 12 months or older.

If a case of measles occurs in your facility:

- Immediately notify the local health department. They will decide if a special immunization program or other treatment is needed for those in close contact with the infected person.
- Exclude the infected person from the facility until 5 days after the rash appears.
- Notify parents. Any unimmunized children and adults should be immunized or excluded from the center until 2 weeks after the rash appears in the last case of measles in the facility.
- Closely observe all children to determine whether any additional cases may be developing.

the **ABC**s
of Safe and Healthy
Child Care

What You Should Know About...
Mumps in the Child Care Setting

Mumps is caused by the mumps virus. Although mumps does not usually cause serious longterm problems, the acute symptoms, such as severe swelling of the salivary glands under the jaw bone, can be very uncomfortable. Adults are more likely to have serious complications if they become infected. Child care providers should be aware that exposure to the virus in the first trimester of pregnancy may increase the rate of spontaneous abortion. Mumps is spread from person to person through direct contact with saliva, secretions from the respiratory tract, and urine of an infected person.

Mumps is vaccine-preventable. Adults born before 1957 are considered to be immune. The mumps vaccine is administered as part of the MMR (measles, mumps, rubella) vaccine series to children beginning at 12 to 15 months and again at 4 to 6 years of age or 11 to 12 years of age.

If a case of mumps occurs in your facility:

- Notify the local health department
- Notify parents.
- Exclude the infected child from the facility until 9 days after the swelling begins, or until the swelling subsides.
- Make sure all children and adults follow good handwashing practices.
- In large facilities, follow appropriate group separation practices.
- Review the immunization records of all children in the facility to assure they have received their first mumps vaccination. Those not adequately vaccinated should be referred to their physicians.
- Closely observe all children for symptoms and refer anyone developing symptoms to his or her physician.

104

the **ABC**s
of Safe and Healthy
Child Care

What You Should Know About...
Pertussis in the Child Care Setting

Pertussis (whooping cough) is a very contagious and dangerous infection of the respiratory tract caused by the bacterium *Bordetella pertussis*. Whooping cough gets its name from the whooping sound the child makes when trying to draw breath after a coughing spell. Not all children with whooping cough make this sound; very young children may not be strong enough. Symptoms generally include those of a cold, such as runny nose and a cough that gradually worsens. Violent coughing spells frequently end with vomiting. Once the whooping stage begins, antibiotics are of no use.

Pertussis is spread from person to person through the air. A person who is not immune to pertussis becomes infected by inhaling air that has been contaminated with the respiratory secretions of an infected person who has coughed.

Before vaccines and antibiotics were developed, pertussis was a common cause of death in young children. Today, it is vaccine preventable. Children in the United States are now immunized with the pertussis vaccine beginning at 2 months of age and again at 4 months, 6 months, 15 months, and 4 to 6 years. All children attending a child care facility should be up to date on vaccinations.

If a child or adult in your facility is diagnosed with pertussis:

- Immediately notify the local health department.
- Exclude the infected person from the facility until that person has been on antibiotics for at least 5 days or for 4 weeks after onset of intense coughing.
- Make sure that all children and staff observe careful handwashing technique.
- In large facilities, follow appropriate group separation as discussed in the chapter, "Following Protective Practices to Reduce Disease and Injury."
- Require up-to-date immunization certificates for all children in your care.
- Carefully monitor all children and staff for coughs. Anyone developing a persistent cough should be immediately referred to his or her physician.

the ABCs
of Safe and Healthy
Child Care

What You Should Know About...
Pinkeye (Conjunctivitis) in the Child Care Setting

Pinkeye, also called conjunctivitis, can be caused by bacterial or viral infections or by allergic reactions to dust, pollen, and other materials. Bacterial and viral infections usually produce a white or yellowish pus that may cause the eyelids to stick shut in the morning. The discharge in allergic conjunctivitis is often clear and watery. All types involve redness and burning or itching eyes. Pinkeye in child care settings is most often due to bacterial or viral infections. It can usually be treated with antibiotics. Red and sore eyes may be part of viral respiratory infections. including measles.

The germs that cause conjunctivitis may be present in nasal secretions, as well as in the discharge from the eyes. Persons can become infected when their hands become contaminated with these materials and they rub their eyes. Eyes can also become infected when a person uses contaminated towels or eye makeup.

If a child in your facility develops pinkeye:

- Contact the child's parents and ask them to have the child seen by the doctor. Eye injuries and foreign bodies in the eye can cause similar symptoms.
- Monitor the other children for signs of developing pinkeye.
- Make sure all children and staff use good handwashing practices and hygiene including proper use and disposal of paper tissues used for wiping nasal secretions.
- Eliminate any shared articles, such as towels. Use disposable paper towels.
- Disinfect any articles that may have been contaminated.
- Exclude children with a white or yellow discharge until they have been treated with an antibiotic for at least 24 hours. Children with a watery discharge generally do not need to be excluded unless there have been other children in the group with similar symptoms, but should be monitored for signs of more serious illness, such as fever or rash.

the **A B C**s
of Safe and Healthy
Child Care

What You Should Know About...
Pinworms in the Child Care Setting

Pinworms are tiny parasitic worms that live in the large intestine. The female worms lay their eggs around the anus at night. Symptoms include anal itching, sleeplessness, irritability, and anal irritation due to scratching. Pinworms may also be present without symptoms. Pinworms are common in school-aged children.

Pinworms are spread when an uninfected person touches the anal area of an infected person (e.g., during diaper changing) or sheets or other articles contaminated with pinworm eggs, then touches the mouth, transferring the eggs, and swallows the eggs. An infected person can spread pinworms by scratching the anal area, then contaminating food or other objects which are then eaten or touched by uninfected persons. Pinworms can be spread as long as either worms or eggs are present. Eggs can survive up to 2 weeks away from a human host.

To prevent the spread of pinworms:

- If you suspect a child has pinworms, call the parents and ask them to have the child diagnosed.
- Exclude a child with pinworms from the child care facility until 24 hours after the the child has seen a physician and received the first treatment. The entire family may have to be treated to prevent reinfection.
- Observe proper handwashing among children and adults, particularly before eating and after using the toilet.
- Clean and disinfect bathroom surfaces.
- Vacuum carpeted areas.
- Machine wash bed linens and hand towels using **hot water**. Machine dry using a **heat setting** (not air fluff). The family should do the same at home.
- Require that the nails of all children in your care be kept short and discourage nail biting.
- Discourage children from scratching the anal area.
- Parents should be asked to make sure that the child is bathed after treatment and just before returning to child care. This will help remove any eggs that were laid around the anus before treatment.

the **ABC**s
of Safe and Healthy
Child Care

What You Should Know About...
Polio in the Child Care Setting

Polio is caused by the poliovirus. It gains entry to the body by fecal-oral spread and can infect the intestinal tract. It can be excreted and may be spread through the feces. Polio attacks the nervous system and can cause paralysis in legs or other parts of the body. Polio is still common in other parts of the world where many people remain unvaccinated.

Because of widespread use of polio vaccine, the United States has not had a naturally occurring case of polio in over 10 years. However, the polio vaccine uses a weakened virus that can be spread from people who have received the vaccine to people who are not immune. Eight to 10 cases of polio are reported each year associated with the vaccine virus, and half of these cases are among persons who have contact with someone who has recently been vaccinated.

All children should be immunized against polio with doses of the oral polio vaccine at 2, 4, and 6 months and at 4 to 6 years of age. When children are vaccinated using live polio vaccine, they may shed live polio vaccine virus in their saliva or feces for several weeks after receiving the vaccine. Anyone who is in frequent contact with recently vaccinated children, especially changing diapers, should be certain they have been vaccinated against polio. Anyone who is not immune to polio or whose immune system is compromised for any reason, such as persons on chemotherapy for cancer, persons with HIV infection or AIDS, or pregnant women, should not have contact with the saliva or feces of a person who may be shedding polio vaccine virus. To avoid the risk of exposing immune deficient persons to live polio vaccine virus, persons with normal immune systems who share the same household may be immunized with an inactivated ("killed") poliovaccine. Persons with immune deficiency should avoid contact with diapered children who have been immunized for at least 1 month after the immunization. Following good handwashing technique after changing children's diapers is essential in preventing transmission of the vaccine virus after children have been immunized.

108

the ABCs
of Safe and Healthy
Child Care

What You Should Know About...
Respiratory Syncytial Virus (RSV) in the Child Care Setting

RSV causes infections of the upper respiratory tract (like a cold) and the lower respiratory tract (like pneumonia). It is the most frequent cause of lower respiratory infections, including pneumonia, in infants and children under 2 years of age. Almost 100 percent of children in child care get RSV in the first year of their life, usually during outbreaks during the winter months. In most children, symptoms appear similar to a mild cold. About half of the infections result in lower respiratory tract infections and otitis media. An RSV infection can range from very mild to life-threatening or even fatal. Children with heart or lung disease and weak immune systems are at increased risk of developing severe infection and complications. RSV causes repeated symptomatic infections throughout life.

RSV is spread through direct contact with infectious secretions such as by breathing them in after an infected person has coughed or by touching a surface an infected person has contaminated by touching it or coughing on it. A young child with RSV may be infectious for 1 to 3 weeks after symptoms subside.

The most effective preventive measure against the spread of RSV and other respiratory viral infections is careful and frequent handwashing. Once one child in a group is infected with RSV, spread to others is rapid. Frequently, a child is infectious before symptoms appear. Therefore, an infected child does not need to be excluded from child care unless he or she is not well enough to participate in usual activities.

If a child or adult in the child care facility develops an illness caused by RSV infection:

- Make sure that procedures regarding handwashing, hygiene, disposal of tissues used to clean nasal secretions, and cleaning and disinfection of toys are followed.
- If multiple cases occur, cohorting or separating ill children from well/recovered children may help to reduce the spread of RSV. Do not exclude ill children unless they are unable to participate comfortably in activities or require a level of care that would jeopardize the health and safety of the other children in your care.

the **ABC**s
of Safe and Healthy
Child Care

What You Should Know About...
Ringworm in the Child Care Setting

Ringworm is a fungus infection of the scalp or skin. Symptoms include a rash that is often itchy and flaky. Ringworm on the scalp may leave a flaky patch of baldness. On other areas of the skin, ringworm causes a reddish, ringlike rash that may itch or burn. The area may be dry and scaly or it may be moist or crusted. The same fungi that infect humans can also infect animals such as dogs and cats, and infections may be acquired from pets as well as from infected children.

Ringworm is spread by direct contact with a person or animal infected with the fungus. It can also be spread indirectly through contact with articles (such as combs or clothing) or surfaces which have been contaminated with the fungus. A child with ringworm is infectious as long as the fungus remains present in the skin lesion. The fungus is no longer present when the lesion starts to shrink.

If you suspect that a child in your facility has ringworm:

- Notify the parents and ask them to contact the child's physician for diagnosis.
- If the lesion cannot be covered, exclude a child with ringworm until after treatment has begun and the lesion has started to shrink.
- Observe good handwashing technique among all children and adults.
- Prohibit sharing of personal items, such as hair care articles, towels, and clothing.
- Dry skin thoroughly after washing.
- Wash bathroom surfaces and toys daily.
- Vacuum carpeted areas and upholstered furniture.

Pets with skin rashes should be evaluated by a veterinarian for evaluation. If the pet's rash is caused by fungus, children should not be allowed to come in contact with the pet until the rash has been treated and heals and the pet has been bathed.

the **ABC**s
of Safe and Healthy
Child Care

What You Should Know About...
Roseola in the Child Care Setting

Roseola (exanthem subitum) is caused by a virus called human herpesvirus 6 (HHV-6) and, possibly, human herpesvirus 7 (HHV-7). It is most common in children 6 months to 24 months of age. Symptoms include a high fever that lasts for 3 to 5 days, runny nose, irritability, eyelid swelling, and tiredness. When the fever disappears, a rash appears, mainly on the face and body, and lasts for about 24 to 48 hours. However, other complications of roseola are rare.

Roseola is spread from person to person, but it is not known how. Roseola is not very contagious. Usually, roseola goes away without any treatment. A child with fever and rash should be excluded from child care until seen by a physician. A child with rash and no fever may return to child care.

the ABCs
of Safe and Healthy
Child Care

What You Should Know About...
Rotavirus Diarrhea in the Child Care Setting

Rotavirus is one type of virus that causes diarrhea, especially in young children. It is a common cause of infection is a common cause of diarrhea in the child care setting. Rotavirus infection usually occurs during the winter months. Some children have no symptoms of rotavirus infection while others may have severe vomiting , watery diarrhea, and fever. In some instances, there may also be a cough or runny nose. Rotavirus diarrhea usually lasts from 4 to 6 days, but may last longer and cause intermittent diarrhea in children who have compromised immune systems.

Rotavirus infections may be highly contagious. Children and adults can become infected by coming in direct contact with the viruses that are in the feces of an infected child and then passing those viruses to the mouth (fecal-oral transmission). Often, another child or adult touches a surface that has been contaminated and then touches his or her mouth. A child with rotavirus infection may be contagious before the onset of diarrhea and for a few days after the diarrhea has ended.

A vaccine for rotavirus is being developed but is not yet available. Although there is no specific therapy for rotavirus diarrhea, the most effective therapy is to encourage ill children to drink plenty of fluids to avoid dehydration.

To prevent the spread of rotavirus infection in your facility:

- Exclude any child with diarrhea from the child care setting until these symptoms are gone.
- Exclude any adult who has diarrhea until these symptoms are gone.
- Make sure that everyone in the child care setting practices good handwashing.
- Wash your hands after using the toilet, helping a child use the toilet, and diapering a child and before preparing or serving food.
- Have children wash their hands upon arrival at your child care facility, after using the toilet, after having their diapers changed (an adult should wash an infant's or small child's hands), and before eating snacks or meals.
- Disinfect toys, diaper changing surfaces, bathrooms, and food preparation surfaces daily.
- Use disposable paper towels for handwashing.
- Parents should contact the child's physician if their child develops diarrhea.

the **ABC**s
of Safe and Healthy
Child Care

What You Should Know About...
Rubella in the Child Care Setting

Rubella, also called German measles or three-day measles, is a very contagious disease caused by the rubella virus. The virus causes fever, swollen lymph nodes behind the ears, and a rash that starts on the face and spreads to the torso and then to the arms and legs. Rubella is no longer very common because most children are immunized beginning at 12 months of age. Rubella is not usually a serious disease in children, but can be very serious if a pregnant woman becomes infected. Infection with rubella in the first 3 months of pregnancy can cause serious injury to the fetus, resulting in heart damage, blindness, deafness, mental retardation, miscarriage, or stillbirth.

Rubella is spread person-to-person by breathing in droplets of respiratory secretions exhaled by an infected person. It may also be spread when someone touches his or her nose or mouth after their hands have been in contact with infected secretions (such as saliva) of an infected person. A person can spread the disease from as many as 5 days before the rash appears to 5 to 7 days after.

Rubella may be prevented by immunization. The rubella vaccine is part of the MMR (measles, mumps, rubella) vaccine series administered to children beginning at 12 months of age.

All child care providers should be immune to rubella. People are considered immune only if they have received at least one dose of Rubella vaccine on or after their first birthday or if they have laboratory evidence of rubella immunity.

If a child or adult in the child care facility develops rubella:

- Exclude the infected child or adult until 6 days after the onset of the rash.
- Notify the local health department immediately.
- Review all immunization records of the children in your care. Any children under 12 months who have not yet been vaccinated against rubella should be excluded until they have been immunized or until 3 weeks after the onset of rash in the last case.
- Refer any pregnant woman who has been exposed to rubella to her doctor.
- Follow good handwashing and hygiene procedures.
- Carefully observe other children, staff, or family members for symptoms.

of Safe and Healthy
Child Care

What you should know about...
Salmonella Infections in the Child Care Setting

The Salmonella group of bacteria are a common cause of diarrheal illness among persons in the United States. These bacteria are often found in the digestive tract of a variety of animals as well as humans. Persons with salmonella infections often experience fever, stomach cramps, nausea and vomiting in addition to diarrhea. Symptoms may persist for two weeks or more but are usually gone within a week.

Salmonella is present in the feces of ill and recently recovered persons and infections may be spread from person to person. However, outbreaks in child care settings are rare and most persons are believed to have acquired their infections from contaminated food. Some foods, such as chicken, come from naturally infected sources while others (such as tomatoes and some vegetables) are contaminated during processing. Food handlers may also contaminate food if they are infected or do not practice good hygiene in preparing food. An ordinarily safe food, such as baked goods, may become contaminated from juices of uncooked foods such as poultry. Although it has been known that salmonella may be present in cracked eggs for some time, it has been only recently that salmonella has been found in uncooked whole eggs. Given sufficient moisture and temperatures between 40° and 140° C, small numbers of salmonella will quickly increase to the point where they can cause illness in large numbers of persons. In addition to foodborne illnesses, pets, especially animals such as turtles, lizards and birds, often carry salmonella in their digestive tracts.

While child care providers are most likely to encounter this condition as a result of infection outside their facility, they need to be aware of good hygiene and foodhandling practices to prevent foodborne illness from occurring within their facility. Additionally, providers may reduce the likelihood of salmonella infection by:

- Making sure that children wash their hands after handling animals and cleaning their cages or pens. Because of the risk of salmonella infection, turtles, lizards, and other reptiles should not be kept as pets in child care centers.
- Limiting the serving of snacks and treats prepared outside the facility and served for special occasions to those from commercial sources. Home-prepared snacks may be not only prepared under less than optimal circumstances but may be transported and stored under conditions that will allow bacteria to grow. Avoid food containing raw eggs, including homemade ice cream made with raw eggs.
- Make sure that lunches brought from home are refrigerated when necessary. These include meals containing raw vegetables as well as those with meats. Dairy products and liquid formula should also be kept refrigerated in order to limit the growth of bacteria, including salmonella.
- Notify your state or local health department if you become aware that a child or staff person in your facility is infected with salmonella.

the
A
B **C** s
of Safe and Healthy
Child Care

What You Should Know About...
Scabies in the Child Care Setting

Scabies is caused by a tiny mite, *Sarcoptes scabiei*, that burrows into the skin, causing a rash. The rash is usually found on the wrists, elbows, or between the fingers. In infants, the rash may appear on the head, neck, or body.

Scabies is spread by skin-to-skin contact. Because mites can survive only briefly if not on the human body, you can only get scabies from direct contact with another person or by sharing an infected person's clothes. Over-the-counter insecticide lotion treatments are available for killing the mites. Young children suspected of having scabies should see a physician, as should persons with extensive skin disease. If scabies is diagnosed in either a child or adult in your facility:

- Exclude the person until 24 hours after treatment has been completed.
- Notify any other adults or the parents of children who may have had direct contact with the infected person. Other providers and children and their families may have been infected and may need treatment. The rash may take 2 to 6 weeks to develop in persons who have not had scabies previously. If a person has had scabies previously, it will take only days for the rash to develop.
- To treat scabies,
    - --Bathe thoroughly.
    - --Apply the lotion from neck to toes for the designated length of time.
    - --Bathe again.
    - --Wash all clothes. bedding, and towels used by the infected person in hot water and dry them in a hot dryer.
    - --Monitor the infected person. A second treatment may be needed a week later.

the **ABC**s
of Safe and Healthy
Child Care

What You Should Know About...

Shigellosis in the Child Care Setting

Shigellosis is a diarrheal illness caused by the Shigella group of bacteria. Infection is spread by the fecal-oral route. Only a few bacteria are needed to cause an infection and, unlike many of the diarrheal agents in child care settings, *shigella* may spread through groups of children who are toilet trained as well as through groups of children who are in diapers.

Depending on the infectious dose, infection with shigella may be very mild or it may result in severe bloody diarrhea, fever, cramping, nausea and vomiting. Numerous outbreaks have been reported from child care settings. Children may spread infections acquired in child care facilities to their parents and siblings and whole families may be ill within a matter of days. Deaths have been reported from this illness and it is one of the more serious infections providers are likely to encounter in the child care setting.

If you suspect a case of shigellosis in your child care facility:

- Contact your state or local health department. Prompt intervention may help prevent the spread of shigellosis to others and your health department should be in a position to give assistance and advice.
- Exclude the ill child and any children who subsequently develop diarrhea from child care until they no longer have diarrhea and have been shown to be free of the *shigella* bacteria. In many areas, public health regulations require proof that an infected person is no longer excreting *shigella* bacteria before they can return to their normal activities. Your health department should be able to tell you when infected persons can return to child care.
- Make sure all children and adults use careful handwashing and that staff are practicing good diapering practices.
- Make sure procedures for cleaning and disinfecting toys are being followed; that toys are being cleaned and disinfected between use by children who are likely to put them in their mouths, especially in groups where there have been ill children.
- Notify parents of children in the involved classroom of the illness, ask that they have any child with diarrhea, vomiting or severe cramping evaluated by a physician and that they inform you of diarrheal illness in their child and family. Explain to them the value of handwashing with soap and running water in stopping the spread of infection in the home. In the event of an outbreak, your health department may recommend a more extensive notification of parents.

the **ABC**s
of Safe and Healthy
Child Care

What You Should Know About...
Strep Throat and Scarlet Fever in the Child Care Setting

Strep throat is caused by group A Streptococcus bacteria. Strep throat is more common in children than in adults. Strep throat is easily spread when an infected person coughs or sneezes contaminated droplets into the air and another person inhales them. A person can also get infected from touching these secretions and then touching their mouth or nose.

Symptoms of strep throat infections may include severe sore throat, fever, headache, and swollen glands. If not treated, strep infections can lead to scarlet fever, rheumatic fever, skin, bloodstream, ear infections, and pneumonia. Scarlet fever is characterized by a bright red, rough textured rash that spreads all over the child's body. Rheumatic fever is a serious disease that can damage the heart valves.

If you suspect a case of strep throat in your child care facility:

- Call the parents to pick up the child and have her or him evaluated by a health care professional.
- Request that the parents inform you if the child is diagnosed with strep so that you can carefully observe the other children for symptoms of sore throat and fever and notify other parents to closely observe their children.
- A child diagnosed with strep throat may return to the child care facility 24 hours after the child has been on antibiotic therapy for at least 24 hours and if he or she has had no fever for 24 hours.

the ABCs
of Safe and Healthy
Child Care

What You Should Know About...

Sudden Infant Death Syndrome (SIDS) in the Child Care Setting

SIDS is a term used to describe the sudden, unexplained death of an infant that *remains* unexplained after a thorough case investigation that includes a complete autopsy, an examination of the death scene, and a review of the clinical history. SIDS is the leading cause of death of children 1 month to 1 year of age. In the United States, 5,000 to 6,000 infant deaths are attributed to SIDS each year. Many of these occur in the child care setting.

The cause of SIDS is unknown. SIDS is not contagious. SIDS is not caused by vomiting, choking, or minor illnesses such as colds or infections. Deaths due to vaccine reactions or child abuse are not classified as SIDS deaths. While we don't know what *causes* SIDS, we have identified four factors *associated with increased risk* of SIDS: (1) placing a baby on the stomach (prone position) to sleep; (2) being exposed to tobacco smoke during pregnancy and after birth; (3) using soft surfaces and objects that trap air or gases, such as pillows, in a baby's sleeping area; and (4) not breastfeeding a baby. However, risk factors alone do not cause SIDS. Most babies with one or more of the above risk factors do not succumb to SIDS.

To *decrease the risk* of SIDS in the child care setting:
- Place babies on their backs or side to sleep. This recommendation from the American Academy of Pediatrics and the National Back to Sleep Campaign applies to most babies. However, some babies should lie in a prone position, such as those with respiratory disease, symptomatic gastro-esophageal reflux, or certain upper airway malformations. If uncertain about a baby's best sleeping position, consult the baby's parents or doctor.
- Don't smoke; provide a smoke-free environment for babies in your care; encourage parents who smoke to quit. Recent research indicates that the risk of SIDS *doubles* among babies *exposed only after birth* to cigarette smoke and *triples* for those *exposed both during pregnancy and after birth*.
- Use firm, flat mattresses in safety-approved cribs for babies' sleep. Don't use soft sleeping surfaces and objects that trap gas in the babies' sleeping area. The U.S. Consumer Product Safety Commission has issued advisories for parents on the hazards to infants sleeping on beanbag cushions, sheepskins, foam pads, foam sofa cushions, synthetic-filled adult pillows, and foam pads covered with comforters.

- Encourage mothers who breastfeed to provide you with bottled breastmilk that is clearly labeled with their child's name. Studies show that babies who died of SIDS were less likely to have been breastfed. Breastfeeding prevents gastrointestinal and respiratory illnesses and infections.

If a child in your care is not breathing and is unresponsive:
- Call 911.
- Begin cardiopulmonary resuscitation (CPR).
- Immediately notify emergency medical personnel (dial 911).
- Immediately notify the child's parents.

If a child in your care dies:
- Do not disturb the scene of death (i.e., don't move anything), if possible.
- Contact your emergency child care backup person to tend to the other children.
- Document the entire sequence of events.
- Prepare to talk with law enforcement officers, a coroner or medical examiner, and licensing and insurance agencies.
- Notify the parents of the other children in your care of the death. You may later need to provide additional information regarding the death.

If the death of a child in your care is attributed to SIDS:
- Seek support and SIDS information from your local health department of from local, state, or national SIDS resources.
- For inquiries or to request materials, call "Back to Sleep" at 1-800-505-CRIB or write "Back to Sleep" at P.O. Box 29111, Washington, DC 20040.
- Obtain a copy of "When Sudden Infant Death Syndrome (SIDS) Occurs in Childcare Settings...", contact the National Sudden Infant Death Syndrome Resource Center, 8201 Greensboro Drive, Suite 600, McLean, Virginia 22102-3810. Telephone: (703) 821-8955; Facsimile: (703) 821-2098.
- Provide the parents of other children in your care information on SIDS that is appropriate for them and for their children.

For further support, contact the Sudden Infant Death Syndrome Alliance, 10500 Little Patuxent Parkway, Suite 420, Columbia, Maryland 21044. Telephone: 1-(800) 221-7437 or (301) 964-8000.

the A B Cs
of Safe and Healthy
Child Care

What You Should Know About...

Tetanus in the Child Care Setting

Tetanus, also called lockjaw, is very rare in the United States due to the very high immunization rates of persons living here. Tetanus is difficult to treat, but is completely preventable through vaccination. Children receive tetanus vaccine in combination with the pertussis and diphtheria vaccine. After childhood, adults need a booster injection every 10 years to make sure they are protected.

Tetanus is caused by infection with the bacteria *Clostridium tetani*. These bacteria are common in the soil but are quickly killed by oxygen. Any wound or cut contaminated with the soil and not open to the air (such as a puncture wound or even a rose prick) will provide a suitable environment for the bacteria. Tetanus is usually acquired when a person who has not been immunized acquires such a wound by stepping on a dirty nail or being cut by a dirty tool. The bacteria infect the wound and produce a toxin that spreads through the blood. This toxin can cause severe muscle spasms, paralysis, and frequently death.

Anyone who has an open wound injury should determine the date of his or her last tetanus booster. A person who has not had a booster within the past 10 years, should receive a booster dose of vaccine and/or other medications to prevent tetanus disease. For some wounds, a person may need a booster if more than 5 years have elapsed since the last dose. Because tetanus is not spread person-to-person, tetanus in one child care attendee or provider will not spread to others.

the **ABC**s
of Safe and Healthy
Child Care

What You Should Know About...
Tuberculosis (TB) in the Child Care Setting

TB is a disease caused by bacteria called *Mycobacterium tuberculosis*. These germs can be spread from one person to others. These germs can be spread through the air when a person with TB disease coughs, sneezes, yells, or sings. Children, although they may be infectious, usually are not as likely as adults to transmit TB to others. (TB is not spread by objects such as clothes, toys, dishes, walls, floors, and furniture.) When a person is sick from the TB germ, the person has TB disease. TB can be serious for anyone, but is especially dangerous for children younger than 5 years old and for any persons who have weak immune systems, such as those with HIV infection or AIDS.

You should know the difference between the two stages of TB: (1) **TB infection** is just having the TB germ in the body without being sick, and (2) **active TB or TB disease** is having the germ and also being sick from it, with the symptoms of active TB (see description of symptoms below).

When a child has TB infection, it means that the child was infected by an adult with active TB--often a person in the home. Most persons who have TB infection do not know it because it does not make them sick. A person with only TB infection cannot spread TB to others and does not pose an immediate danger to the public. TB infection is diagnosed only by the TB skin test. This safe, simple test is given at most local health departments. A small injection is made under the skin, usually on the forearm. In persons who are infected with the TB germ, the skin test causes a firm swelling in the skin where the test was given. After 1 or 2 days, a health care provider reads the results of the TB skin test.

A TB-infected person can take 6 to 12 months of medicine, usually isoniazid, to get rid of the TB germs and to prevent **active TB** (the illness with symptoms). This preventive treatment is most important for TB-infected children younger than 5 years old, persons infected with the TB germ within the past 2 years, and TB-infected persons who have a weak immune system (especially HIV infection or AIDS) because these persons are more likely to get active TB after infection.

Active TB (when infection develops into a disease with symptoms) is preventable and curable. Active TB can attack any part of the body, but it usually affects the lungs. Persons with active TB in the lungs may spread TB germs through the air by coughing, sneezing, or yelling. People who share this air have a chance of breathing in the germs and getting the infection in their lungs, too.

Persons with active TB have symptoms such as a cough that "won't go away," a cough that brings up blood, a fever lasting longer than 2 weeks, night sweats, feeling very tired, or losing a noticeable amount of weight. The TB skin test cannot show active TB -- active TB must be diagnosed by a physician, based on a physical exam, a chest x-ray, and laboratory tests. The treatment for active TB usually involves taking at least 3 different drugs and lasts for at least 6 months and usually cures the TB. The law states that doctors must report active TB to the local health department.

In child care settings, TB has been spread from adults to children, although the spread of TB in such settings is rare. In family home child care settings, TB infection has been passed from sick adults living in the home to children, even thought the sick adults may not have been taking care of the children directly. As noted before, a person with only TB infection cannot infect another person. Only a person with active TB can infect another person. Also, children younger than 5 years old who have active TB usually cannot infect other persons. The spread of TB from child to child in a child care setting has not been reported. Still, children under 5 years old who have active TB should not attend child care until they have been given permission. Usually, they may return to child care as soon as they are feeling well and on medication, but this should be decided by the local health department. (Well children should not be kept out of child care if they only have a positive skin test result.)

In the United States, TB is more common in some populations, for example immigrants coming from Asia, Africa, and Latin America and medically underserved minority populations. However, overall, TB infection in children younger than 5 years old is rare. Therefore, TB skin testing of all children in child care centers is not useful. However, a local health department may decide to test children who have more risk for infection. Some programs (e.g., Head Start) and some states require children to have a TB skin test before they can attend. A child who has a positive skin test result should be seen by a doctor to check for active TB and to start medicine that will prevent TB disease, if appropriate. A child should not be kept out of child care only because of a positive TB skin test result.

Persons who are beginning work as a child care provider should have a TB skin test to check for infection with TB bacteria. See the section on health history and immunization policy for child care providers for more information on tuberculosis screening for child care providers. Child care providers who comes from a community with high rates of TB may want to take preventive medicine so they will not develop active TB. Local health department TB control programs can help with these activities.

122

the **ABC**s
of Safe and Healthy
Child Care

What You Should Know About...
Yeast Infections (Thrush) in the Child Care Setting

Yeast infections are caused by various species of *Candida*, especially *Candida albicans*. These organisms are part of the germs normally found in various parts of the body and ordinarily do not cause any symptoms. Certain conditions, such as antibiotic use or excessive moisture, may upset the balance of microbes and allow an overgrowth of *Candida*. In most persons, these infections flare up and then heal. However, in newborns or persons with weak immune systems, this yeast can cause more serious or chronic infections.

Many infants acquire *Candida* infections from their mothers during birth. Many of those that escape this infection soon acquire *Candida* from close contacts with other family members and doting relatives and friends. These early exposures may result in an oral infection (thrush) that appears as creamy white, curd-like patches on the tongue and inside of the mouth. In older persons, treatment with certain types of antibiotics or inhaled steroids (for asthma) may upset the balance of microbes in the mouth, allowing an overgrowth of *Candida* that will also result in thrush. Outbreaks of thrush in child care settings may be the result of increased use of antibiotics rather than newly acquired *Candida* infections.

Candida may also exacerbate diaper rash, as this yeast grows readily on damaged skin. The infected skin is usually fiery red with lesions that may have a raised red border. Children who suck their thumbs or other fingers may occasionally develop *Candida* around their fingernails.

Oral thrush and *Candida* diaper rash are usually treated with the antibiotic nystatin. A corticosteroid cream can be applied to highly inflamed skin lesions on the hands or diaper areas. For children with diaper rash, child care providers should change the diaper frequently, gently clean the child's skin with water and a mild soap and pat dry. While cornstarch or baby powder may be recommended for mild diaper rash, it should not be used for children with inflamed skin. High absorbency disposable diapers may help keep the skin dry. Plastic pants that do not allow air to circulate over the diaper area should not be used although the diapering system should be able to hold urine or liquid feces.

Since most persons are already infected with *Candida*, children with thrush and candida diaper rash need not be excluded from child care as long they are able to participate comfortably. Child care providers should follow good hygiene including careful handwashing and disposal of nasal and oral secretions of children with thrush in order to avoid transmitting the infection to children who are not already infected.

ADDITIONAL RESOURCES

FEDERAL AGENCIES

Agency	For Information On	Call
Agency for Toxic Substances and Disease Registry 1600 Clifton Road, N.E., MS-E60 Atlanta, Georgia 30333	Chemical spills and accidental releases Chemical poisoning emergencies Educational materials Hazardous waste sites (EPA hotline) Toxic effects of individual chemicals	404-639-6360 Poison Control Center 404-639-6204 202-260-0056 404-639-6300
Centers for Disease Control and Prevention Child Care Health and Safety Program, MS-A07 1600 Clifton Road, N.E., Atlanta, Georgia 30333	Child care health and safety practices Public inquiries on specific diseases	404-639-6475 404-639-3534
Consumer Product Safety Commission	Public playground safety and *Handbook for Public Playground Safety*	301-504-0580
Department of Energy and the National Institute of Environmental Health Sciences, NIH	Electric and magnetic fields Contact the US Government Printing Office and ask for publication DOE/EE-0040	202-512-1800 (USGPO)
Environmental Protection Agency Office of Radiation and Indoor Air, MS-66045 401 M Street, SW, Washington, DC 20406	Radiation and indoor air pollution	202-233-9438
Maternal and Child Health Bureau Health Resources and Services Administration 5600 Fishers Lane, Rm.A-39, Rockville, MD 20857	Maternal and child health	301-443-6600
National AIDS Clearinghouse	AIDS prevention, treatment, etc., inquiries	800- 458-5231

Agency	For Information On	Call
National Alcohol and Drug Abuse Clearinghouse	Substance abuse prevention, treatment, etc., inquiries and to order publications	800- 729-6686
National Institute of Child Health and Development 9000 Rockville Pike, Bethesda, MD 20892	Child health and development	
National Highway Transportation Safety Administration Auto Safety Hotline	Recalls on child car seats; Have brand name, model number, manufacturing date ready.	800- 424-9393

ORGANIZATIONS

Organization	For Information On	Call

American Academy of Pediatrics
141 N. Westpoint Boulevard
Elk Grove, Illinois 60007
	To order publications
	To obtain "Parent Resource Guide" listing publications available, send a self-addressed, stamped envelope to:
	    AAP, Department C
	    P.O.Box 927
	    Elk Grove, Illinois 60009-0927
		847-228-5005

American Public Health Association 1015 15th Street, Washington, DC 20005	Health and child care inquiries To order publications	202-789-5600 202-789-5667
American Red Cross National Headquarters Health and Safety 18th and F Streets, NW, Washington, DC 20006	Cardiopulmonary resuscitation Child care course	Local chapter (listed in telephone book)
Asian Pacific Islander American Health Forum 116 New Montgomery, Suite 531 San Francisco, CA 94105	Issues affecting Asian Pacific Islanders	415-541-0866
"Back to Sleep" P.O. Box 29111, Washington, DC 20040	SIDS prevention	800- 505-CRIB
Child Care Action Campaign 330 Seventh Avenue, 17th Floor New York, New York 10001	Need for child care	212-239-0138
Child Care Aware	Local child care referral organizations and child care issues	800- 424-2246

Organization	For Information On	Call
Child Care Information Center 301 Maple Avenue West, Suite 601 Vienna, VA 22180	General information on child care	800-616-2242
Child Care Law Center 22 Second Street, San Francisco, CA 94105	Legal rights of children in child care, including the Americans with Disabilities Act Answers questions Tuesdays and Thursdays between 9am-12pm PST	415- 495-5498
Child Welfare League of America 440 First Street, NW, Suite 310 Washington, DC 20001-2085	Child care, child abuse, etc. questions To obtain a catalog or order publications	202-638-2085 800-407-6273
Children's Defense Fund 25 E Street, NW, Washington, DC 20001	Child advocacy issues, child care, child welfare questions and statistical information or to obtain a catalog or order publications or merchandise	202-628-8787
Children's Environmental Health Network 5900 Hollis Street, Suite E Emeryville, California 94608	Preventing toxic exposures in children	510-450-3729
Corporate Fund for Children National Latino Children's Institute 611 W. 6th Street, Austin, TX 78703	Latino children's issues--child care, child health border town issues, rural child care, and research. "Fax Back" Info; "Find Out" Clearinghouse, "Latino Professional Network"	512-472-9971

Organization	For Information On	Call
ERIC Clearinghouse on Elementary and Early Childhood Education, University of Illinois 805 W. Pennsylvania Avenue, Urbana, IL 61801-4897	Child education and development	217-333-1386
Families and Work Institute 330 Seventh Avenue, 14th Floor New York, New York 10001	Studies on child care	212-465-2044
National Association for the Education of Young Children 1509 16th Street, NW, Washington, DC 20036-1426	Early childhood education and development Questions and to order publications	202-232-8777 800-424-2460
National Association for Family Child Care	Providing child care in your home Inquiries: Accreditation: Membership services, sales, publications, finances: Insurance: Newsletter:	800-359-3817 817-831-5095 602-838-3446 913-266-5330 609-354-8729
National Association of Child Care Resource and Referral Agencies 1319 F Street, NW, Suite 606 Washington, DC 20004	Regulations affecting child, statistics, children's groups, etc.	202-393-5501
National Black Child Development Institute 1025 15th Street, NW, Washington, DC 20005	Issues affecting African-American children	202-387-1281

Organization	For Information On	Call
National Center for Early Childhood Workforce Childhood Workforce 733 15th Street, NW Suite 1037 Washington, DC 20005	Issues concerning childcare providers—pay, working conditions, "Worthy Wage Campaign"	202-737-7700
National Center for Education in Maternal and Child Health, Georgetown University 2000 Fifteenth Street North, Suite 701 Arlington, VA 22201-2617	Child and maternal health and development	703-524-7802
National Lead Information Hotline	Lead poisoning inquiries	800-LEAD-FYI
National Lead Information Clearinghouse Clearinghouse	Lead poisoning publications and information	800-424-LEAD
National Maternal and Child Health Clearinghouse 2070 Chain Bridge Road, Suite 450 Vienna, VA 22182	Guidelines for child care and other information on child health and development, including the National Guidelines (One copy at no charge)	703-821-8955, ext. 254
National Program for Playground Safety University of Northern Iowa, School of Health Physical Education and Leisure Services Cedar Falls, Iowa 50614-0161	Playground safety	800-554-PLAY (7529)
National Radon Hotline	Radon information in English in Spanish	800-SOS-RADON 800-SALUD-1-2

Organization	For Information On	Call
National Sudden Infant Death Syndrome Resource Center 8201 Greensboro Drive, Suite 600 McLean, VA 22102-3810	SIDS information	703-821-8955
National Technical Information Service 5285 Port Royal Road Springfield, VA 22161	CDC videotape on handwashing and diapering; handwashing poster (multiple copies) (order with credit card)	800-CDC-1824
Public Health Foundation 1220 L Street, NW, Suite 350 Washington, DC 20005	Information on public health issues To order CDC videotape on handwashing and diapering; handwashing poster (single copies)	202-898-5600 800-41TRAIN
Save the Children 1447 Peachtree Street, NE, Suite 700 Atlanta, GA 30309	Child care resource and referral and technical assistance for providers	404-885-1578
Sudden Infant Death Syndrome Alliance 10500 Little Patuxent Parkway, Suite 420 Columbia, MD 21044	SIDS prevention information	800-221-7437 301-964-8000
YMCA 10114 Sunbrook Drive, Beverly Hills, CA 90210	YMCA child care	310-285-0835

Regional Poison Control Centers

ALABAMA
Birmingham
> Children's Hospital of Alabama Poison
> Control Center
> 205-939-9201
> 800-292-6678 (in state)
> 205-933-4050

ARIZONA
Phoenix
> Samaritan Regional Poison Center
> 602-253-3334

Tuscon
> Arizona Poison and Drug Information Center
> 800-362-0101 (in state)
> 602-626-6016

CALIFORNIA
Fresno
> Fresno Regional Poison Control Center
> 209-445-1222

Orange
> UCI Regional Poison Center
> 714-634-5988
> 800-544-4404 (Southern CA only)

Sacramento
> UCDMC Regional Poison Control Center
> 800-342-9293 (Northern CA only)
> 916-734-3692

San Diego
> San Diego Regional Poison Control Center
> 619-543-6000
> 800-876-4766 (619 area code only)

San Francisco
> SF Bay Area Regional Poison Control Center
> 800-523-2222 (7077, 415, and 510 area
> codes only)

San Jose
> Santa Clara Valley Medical Center Regional
> Poision Center
> 408-299-5112
> 800-662-9886 (CA only)

COLORADO
Denver
> Rocky Mountain Poison and Drug Center
> 303-629-1123

DISTRICT OF COLUMBIA
Washington
> National Capitol Poison Control Center
> 202-625-3333
> 202-784-4660 (TTY)

FLORIDA
Tampa
> Florida Poison Information Center
> 800-282-3171 (in state)
> 813-253-4444

GEORGIA
Atlanta
> Georgia Poison Center
> 800-282-5846 (in state)
> 404-589-4400

INDIANA
Indianapolis
> 800-382-9097 (in state)
> 317-929-2323

KENTUCKY
Louisville
> Kentucky Regional Poison Center of
> Kosair Children's Hospital
> 800-722-5725 (in state)
> 502-629-7275

MARYLAND
Baltimore
> Maryland Poison Center
> 800-492-2414 (in state)
> 410-528-7701

MASSACHUSETTS
Boston
> Massachusetts Poison Control System
> 800-682-9211 (in state)
> 617-232-2120

POISON CONTROL CENTERS (CONT.)

MICHIGAN
Detroit
> Poison Control Center
> 313-745-5711

Grand Rapids
> Blodgett Regional Poison Center
> 800-632-2727 (in state)
> 800-356-3232 (TTY)

MINNESOTA
Minneapolis
> Hennepin Regional Poison Center
> 612-347-3141
> 612-337-7474 (TDD)
> 612-337-7387 (Petline)

St. Paul
> Minnesota Regional Poison Center
> 612-221-2113

MISSOURI
St. Louis
> Cardinal Glennon Children's Hospital
> 800-366-8888
> 314-772-5200

MONTANA
Denver (Colorado)
> Rocky Mountain Poison and Drug Center
> 303-629-1123

NEBRASKA
Omaha
> The Poison Center
> 402-390-5555 (Omaha only)
> 800-955-9119 (in state)

NEW JERSEY
Newark
> New Jersey Poison Information and
> Education System
> 800-962-1253 (in state)

NEVADA
Las Vegas
> Rocky Mountain Poison and Drug Center
> 303-629-1123

NEW MEXICO
Albuquerque
> New Mexico Poison and Drug Information
> Center
> 800-432-6866 (in state)
> 505-843-2551

NEW YORK
East Meadow
> Long Island Regional Poison Control Center
> 516-542-2323, 2324, 2325, 3813

New York
> New York City Poison Center
> 212-340-4494
> 212-764-7667
> 212-689-9014 (TDD)

OHIO
Cincinnati
> Regional Poison Control System and
> Cincinnati Drug and Poison Information
> Center
> 513-558-5111
> 800-872-5111 (in state)

Columbus
> Central Ohio Poison Center
> 800-682-7625
> 614-228-1323
> 614-228-2272 (TTY)

OREGON
Portland
> Oregon Poison Center
> 503-494-8968
> 800-452-7165 (in state)

PENNSYLVANIA
Philadelphia
> Poison Control Center
> 215-386-2100 or 2111

Pittsburgh
> Pittsburgh Poison Center
> 412-681-6669

RHODE ISLAND
Providence
> Rhode Island Poison Center
> 401-444-5727

POISON CONTROL CENTERS (CONT.)

TEXAS
Dallas
>North Texas Poison Center
>214-590-5000

UTAH
Salt Lake City
>Intermountain Regional Poison Control
>Center
>801-581-2151
>800-456-7707 (in state)

VIRGINIA
Charlottesville
>Blue Ridge Poison Center
>804-925-5543
>800-451-1428

WASHINGTON, D.C.
>National Capital Poison Center (Northern
>VA only)
>202-625-3333
>202-784-4660 (TTY)

WEST VIRGINIA
Charleston
>West Virginia Poison Center
>800-642-3625 (in state)
>304-348-4211

WYOMING
Omaha (Nebraska)
>The Poison Center
>402-390-5555 (Omaha)
>800-955-9119 (from Wyoming only)

BIBLIOGRAPHY

American Academy of Pediatrics, Committee on Infectious Diseases. *1994 Red Book: Report of the Committee on Infectious Diseases.* Elk Grove Village, IL: American Academy of Pediatrics, 1994.

American Public Health Association and American Academy of Pediatrics under a grant from the U.S. Health Resources and Services Administration. *Caring for Our Children—National Health and Safety Performance Standards: Guidelines for Out-of-Home Child Care Programs.* Washington, DC: APHA & APA, 1992. Also edited and published in 3-ring binder format by the Georgetown University's National Center for Education in Maternal and Child Health, Arlington, VA.

Benenson, A.S., ed. *Control of Communicable Diseases Manual.* Washington, DC: American Public Health Association, 1995.

Canadian Paediatric Society. *Well Beings: A Guide to Promote the Physical Health, Safety and Emotional Well-Being of Children in Child Care Centres and Family Day Care Homes.* Toronto, Ontario: Creative Premises Ltd., 1992.

Centers for Disease Control. *What You Can Do to Stop Disease in Child Day Care Centers.* Atlanta, GA: Government Printing Office, 1984.

Donowitz, L. G., ed. *Infection Control in the Child Care Center and Preschool.* Baltimore, MD: William & Wilkins, 1993.

Shapiro Kendrick, A., Kaufmann, R. and Messenger, K.P., eds. *Healthy Young Children.* Washington, DC: National Association for the Education of Young Children, 1995.

134

INDEX

136